Activism in Pursuit of the Public Interest

Activism in Pursuit of the Public Interest: The Jurisprudence of Chief Justice Roger J. Traynor

Ben Field

Published by Berkeley Public Policy Press for the
California Supreme Court Historical Society

Institute of Governmental Studies • University of California, Berkeley

2003

Library of Congress Cataloging-in-Publication Data

Ben Field.
  Activism in pursuit of the public interest : the jurisprudence of Chief Justice Roger J. Traynor / Ben Field
      p. cm.
  Includes bibliographical references.
  ISBN 0-87772-406-7
  1. Traynor, Roger J. 2. Judges--California--Biography. 3. Political questions and judicial power--California--History. I. Title.

  KF373.T69F54 2003
  347.73'14'092--dc21   2003002798

Contents

Acknowledgements

I could not have hoped for a more helpful critic or a more energetic supporter than Harry Scheiber. His advice and encouragement have been indispensable. I am also indebted to Richard Abrams and Robert Kagan, who, like Professor Scheiber, are members of the faculty at the University of California, Berkeley. Their insights made this a better book, and their conversation made this project a wonderful experience.

Many people helped with my research and writing. Don Barrett, John Davies, Richard Jennings, John Junker, Herma Hill Kay, Adrian Kragen, Fred Okrand, and Stephan Riesenfeld generously allowed me to interview them. Their assistance proved invaluable, as did the able librarians at the California State Archives, Boalt Hall, and the Hastings College of the Law. I am fortunate to have found several readers who devoted their time and formidable energy to commenting on my manuscripts. They include Mark Hood, Herma Hill Kay, Charles McClain, and Michael Traynor. This book has also benefited from the scrutiny of Jerry Lubenow and Maria Wolf. Any mistakes in this book are, of course, my own, but thanks to my editors there are far fewer of them. Finally, my wife Nancy made this book possible. Without her support I would not have started and could not have finished.

Foreword

Despite the inexorable nationalization of governmental functions and centralization of authority that America's modern development has produced, the courts of the 50 states continue to play a vital role in ordering our nation's society in virtually all its dimensions. That this is a nation composed of the states as polities and communities, each with its own constitution and not merely with "devolved" powers, remains a core reality and a shaping force in American law. All too often, scholars in the law no less than political scientists and historians— let alone journalists and public intellectuals more generally—give their attention to the courts of the 50 states largely insofar as the decisions of state judges come before the federal courts for review; all too often, the contributions of outstanding individual justices on the state bench receive far less attention, even in the media and the schools of their own states, than is given routinely to federal cases.

The scholarly and public activities of the California Supreme Court Historical Society have been intended to redress this imbalance. One aspect of the Society's efforts has been to expand the scope of legal-history writing on California to embrace the interrelationships of law with society, with the processes of economic change, with politics and ideology and culture. When the Society published its inaugural *Yearbook* volume in 1994, as editor I noted that there was a need for monographic studies on the foregoing themes and a specific deficiency in regard to biography. We lacked biographical studies of individual judges, and many of the most important figures in the state's legal history—even leading justices of the California Supreme Court since 1850—were little studied and little understood. Commenting on that lack, former Chief Justice Malcolm Lucas has written that, "As we grapple today with the scope of the rule of law and the role of our justice system," it is invaluable to have fuller knowledge "about the individuals who crafted the opinions that helped shape our world . . . and the forces that touched them as they reached their decisions." In the present study of the late Chief Justice Roger J. Traynor, the historian and attorney Benjamin Field carries forward in an original and insightful manner the enterprise of historical-biographical study for the California high court.

In any list of the most admired and influential state judges in the nation's history, Traynor stands at the very top level. Perhaps more than any other state judge of his day, Traynor sought explicitly to bring the law into line with the realities of mass (and diverse) society in the modern industrial world. As Field amply demonstrates in this book, Traynor did so under the banner of "judicial creativity." He believed that for courts always to defer passively and mechanically to doctrinal precedent was inconsistent with the great common law tradition, whose essence was the capacity for adaptation, change, and growth. Equally, he believed that it was inconsistent with American ideals regarding democratic governance for the courts to fail in their role as full partners in the process of legal ordering.

Where the court moved in an "activist" mode to institute change, as in the tort revolution that his decisions led—an area of the law in which "creativity" required innovation and doctrinal departures—Traynor built on the great Anglo-American judicial tradition of adaptation rather than perpetuating a mindless faithfulness to rules that no longer were responsive to the realities of modern California society, or doctrines that had produced manifest unfairness. In such instances, the court's innovations could be turned back in a day by a legislature determined to follow a different course of policy. With respect to constitutional decisions, too, Traynor did fearlessly what American courts must do if they are to be effective: Perhaps more than any state judge of his day, Traynor as a scholar and Traynor as a working jurist undertook fearlessly the reconsideration of the central concepts of constitutional law and their adaptation to the realities of the modern world.

In taxation (Traynor's teaching field at Boalt Hall before he went on the bench), in land law, and in conflict of laws, he was brilliant in the ways he applied conventional legal reasoning to produce practical consequences that did not offend modern notions of efficiency, justice, and legality. In family law, race relations, and the processes of the criminal justice system, as Field shows in his detailed and very able studies of these areas of law in the present work, Traynor's innovations blazed the path that other courts, and ultimately the U.S. Supreme Court, would follow. In tort reform, Traynor was of truly unique importance both for his basic jurisprudential methodology and for the results. And yet, as Field is careful to show, for all his contempt for "judicial lethargy," and despite the boldness with which he sought to demonstrate the obsolescence of established but unfair or outmoded (or ridiculous) rules of law, Traynor's pragmatism extended to supporting in a sympathetic way what he saw as the legitimate activities and methods of the executive branch, not least the law enforcement agencies and officers. He did not reject wholesale the *conservative activism* of an earlier generation of judges, nor indeed that of some of his own colleagues on the Court; like others of the best "activist" judges, whether in a conservative or liberal mode, or still other "activists" who were simply difficult to label, Traynor was willing to acknowledge explicitly his penchant for creativity. Still, he was faithful—perhaps without peer in his day—to the requirement that a judge provide a carefully reasoned and clearly crafted opinion in reaching an innovative conclusion. Moreover, he was ever mindful of the heavy responsibility for assuring fairness, for maintaining the health of the law, and for protecting the integrity of the judicial branch. Not least important, historically, is that with able fellow justices who served with him during his long tenure, the California Supreme Court was widely recognized as the most distinguished state bench in America. It was influential in shaping the direction of the law in many other state courts, as well as pointing the way to some major U.S. Supreme Court decisions.

In light, then, of Traynor's signal importance in the development of our law in the modern era, it is most fitting that the California Supreme Court Historical Society should join with the IGS Press of the University of California, Berkeley, to publish this illuminating study of a great American judge.

Harry N. Scheiber
The Stefan Riesenfeld Professor of Law & History, and
Director, Earl Warren Legal Institute
University of California, Berkeley

Introduction

Roger J. Traynor is widely recognized among legal historians as one of the most important American jurists of the twentieth century. When Governor Culbert Olson appointed him to the California Supreme Court in 1940, the Court showed little inclination toward legal reform. That changed during Traynor's 30-year tenure on the Court, primarily because of Traynor. With Traynor in the lead, the four justices Governor Olson appointed dominated the court. Don Barrett, Traynor's clerk and friend, called the period from 1945 to 1956 the "Long Court" because the composition of the Court did not change during that period.[1] It was during the "Long Court" that Traynor gained the reputation as the leading state court judge in the nation.[2] By the time Governor Pat Brown elevated him to chief justice in 1964, Traynor had established himself as the most active advocate for reform on a reformist court. He authored the Court's most innovative and influential decisions, and his jurisprudence remains important today for its impact in several major fields of law.

Traynor's accomplishments were varied. Among the most significant were his judicial decisions on miscegenation, divorce, police searches, and product

---

[1] Interview of Don Barrett by Ben Field, May 24, 1997.

[2] During Traynor's tenure, the California Supreme Court became the most frequently cited court by courts outside of California. A study of these citations showed that 92 percent of the California cases in the study sample were cited at least three times by out-of-state courts. Lawrence Friedman, Robert Kagan, Bliss Cartwright, and Stanton Wheeler, "State Supreme Courts: A Century of Style and Citation," *Stanford Law Review* 33:773, 805 (1981).

liability. His opinion in the 1948 case of *Perez v. Sharpe,* the first judicial decision overturning an antimiscegenation statute, was far ahead of its time. Years
before the civil rights movement had begun to soften longstanding judicial support for racially discriminatory laws and without any significant political cover,
Traynor led the California Supreme Court in rejecting legal prohibitions of interracial marriages. Traynor reformed family law and the doctrines governing those
cases where an interstate conflict of law arose. In the 1952 divorce case of *De-
Burgh v. DeBurgh,* he broke with precedent underlying fault-based divorce. His
opinion in *DeBurgh* laid the conceptual framework for no fault divorce in California, which in turn sparked the "divorce revolution" that swept the country. In
a series of decisions, beginning with *People v. Cahan* in 1955, Traynor restructured the rules for police searches. These decisions dramatically altered the pa-
rameters of police conduct in California and foreshadowed later actions of the
U.S. Supreme Court that applied nationally to police. Finally, Traynor pushed
the Court to adopt a strict liability standard in product defect cases. He first articulated the public interest in holding manufacturers strictly liable for consumer
injuries caused by design or manufacturing defects in his 1949 concurrence in
Escola v. Coca-Cola Bottling Company. Nineteen years later, his opinion in
Greenman v. Yuba Power Products, Inc. gained the unanimous support of his
brethren, making California the first state to adopt a rule of strict product liability.
Strict liability was the most significant doctrinal development in tort law during
the late 20th century.

Traynor embraced the role of judge as policymaker. He viewed judicial activism as a necessity in a fast changing world, and many of his 892 opinions and
75 law review articles offered an intellectual justification for judicial activism.
Few if any theorists of judicial decision making have so resolutely advocated
activism. Even among the great judicial innovators, such as Lemuel Shaw and
Benjamin Cardozo, Traynor was remarkable for his fervent advocacy of judicial
policymaking. His judicial philosophy stands out in the intellectual history of
judging as extreme, yet many of his most innovative opinions gained widespread
acceptance and generated surprisingly little controversy. This is a fascinating
paradox.

Although no complete judicial biography of Traynor has been published to
date, various legal historians have written about Traynor. Most of these commentators have examined, in approving tones, the substantive legal changes he
initiated. Several, notably G. Edward White, who has written the most thorough
analysis of Traynor's judicial thought to date, have also explored Traynor's philosophy of judging. According to White, Traynor's process of decision making

combined reason with intuition.[3] Traynor's writings provide some support for this view. In one passage he wrote,

> Once he [the judge] has marshaled the data pertinent to a controversy, he must articulate a solution that calls for a discriminating sense of which available principle, if any, should govern the case. His task is least complicated when he can choose from among several plausible alternative principles that readily fit the case without looking anachronistic. As the badlands get worse there are clearer indications of what form reclamation might take, though the need remains for judgment of the highest order—that combinations [*sic*] of analysis and intuition culminating in decisions that prove prophetic.[4]

Traynor appears to have used the word "intuition" only this once in describing his decision-making process. The word denotes an absence of rational thought and inference, which seems inconsistent with Traynor's approach to judging. Traynor advocated a scientific approach to judicial policy analysis, and he claimed that judges could conduct that analysis objectively. In the tradition of Louis Brandeis, his opinions took into account social science studies and other sources outside the legal text. His judicial decisions were not the product of intuition. To the contrary, they demonstrated his great confidence in judicial rationalism.

What guided Traynor's scientific approach toward decision making was not intuition, but a cohesive conception of the public interest. He argued explicitly for public policy objectives in his innovative opinions. The arguments and language of those opinions delineated his conception of public interest and revealed the cohesive set of values, preferences, and aversions that underlay it. By treating Traynor's innovative opinions as an ideological exposition, it becomes possible to show his relationship to his ideological environment. Traynor's rhetoric connected *Perez v. Sharpe* with contemporary race relations, *DeBurgh v. DeBurgh* with contemporary conceptions of the role of women, *People v. Cahan* with contemporary attitudes toward law enforcement, and the product liability cases with contemporary views of producer/consumer relations. Understanding the relationships between these cases and their ideological environment is essential to an evaluation of Traynor's work and his influence because the extent to which his policy innovations gained acceptance and became institutionalized in American law depended largely on their resonance with his ideological surroundings.

---

[3]G. Edward White, *The American Judicial Tradition: Profiles of Leading American Jurists* (Oxford, 1976), 295.

[4]Roger Traynor, "Badlands in an Appellate Judge's Realm of Reason," *Utah Law Review* 7:157, 160–61 (1960).

Traynor's efforts at reform did not happen in a doctrinal vacuum. They paralleled other contemporary changes in the law, particularly the "constitutional revolution of 1937," which allowed the expansion of government regulatory power over the economy while creating a new civil liberties jurisprudence. The U.S. Supreme Court of the 1920s and early 1930s had sustained a legal structure that protected private property and struck down popular legislation that imposed regulations on businesses. Initially, the Court's opposition to government regulation of the economy put it at odds with the New Deal. During 1935 and 1936, the Court heard 10 major cases involving New Deal legislation and struck down a New Deal program in eight of those cases. These decisions threatened the core of the New Deal. In response, Franklin D. Roosevelts vilified the Court for protecting entrenched, private economic power and obstructing government efforts to regulate the economy for the public good. Public disapproval of the Court's resistance to the New Deal placed great pressure on the Court, and, ultimately, its dramatic change of course in the wake of FDR's 1937 Court-packing message allowed a massive expansion of government power over the economy.

The Supreme Court did not overturn a single New Deal program after 1937, and during the following decade, it reversed 32 of its earlier decisions.[5] Core New Deal statutes, such as National Industrial Recovery Act and the Agricultural Adjustment Act, gained Court approval when just a few years earlier the Court had invalidated the exercise of federal power under the same statutes. Labor laws mandating collective bargaining and a minimum wage, relief programs, antimonopoly regulations, Social Security, and the host of other New Deal programs passed constitutional muster under the Court's new standards for evaluating economic programs.

While FDR's appointees to the Supreme Court expanded the government's ability to restrict private property rights, they also expanded individual civil rights. As Justice Harlan Stone wrote in a now-famous footnote to his opinion in *United States v. Carolene Products Co.,* the rights enumerated in the Bill of Rights held a "preferred position."[6] In case after case, the Court expanded those rights and held that they applied to the states, reversing longstanding precedent. Under the so-called "second Bill of Rights," constitutional protections for free speech, free exercise of religion, freedom from unreasonable police searches, the right to a free, court-appointed attorney, and the right against self incrimination were the law of the states as well as the law of the federal government. By 1970 the Court had incorporated almost the entire Bill of Rights into the Fourteenth Amendment, thus making it applicable to the states. Despite some backsliding

---

[5]William E. Leuchtenburg, *The Supreme Court Reborn: The Constitutional Revolution in the Age of Roosevelt* (New York, 1995), 233.

[6]United States v. Carolene Products Co., 304 U.S. 144 at 152 n. 4 (1938).

during World War II and the McCarthy era, the "second Bill of Rights" created new protections for political dissenters, religious and racial minorities, and suspected criminals.[7]

The thrust of Traynor's innovative decisions paralleled the "constitutional revolution of 1937." Although he avoided constitutional interpretation in his innovative decisions, gravitating instead to more concrete, policy-oriented analysis, he shared the sympathies of the Courts that expanded civil rights on constitutional grounds. He opposed racially discriminatory laws, laws that perpetuated the inequality of women, and police practices that violated the constitutional rights of suspected criminals. He supported the rights of labor activists and consumers, whom he considered to be economically powerless. In keeping with the "preferred position" doctrine, he generally sided with the government against individual property rights, for instance in eminent domain cases. Traynor acted to reform the law where it preserved power relations he considered unfair, even when it meant striking down longstanding legal precedent. Traynor's concern for society's weak and his willingness to depart from legal convention on their behalf put him in harmony with the dominant currents of legal reform of his day.

Before joining the bench, the central event in Traynor's experience with judicial activism had been the resistance of the U.S. Supreme Court to the New Deal. The triumph of the New Deal over the conservative Court gave judicial activism a new context. Many liberals abhorred the Court's conservative reaction to the New Deal, and they also worried that the triumph of the New Deal over the Court had come at the expense of politicizing the Court.[8] Traynor was uncomfortable with the style of activism that yielded sweeping rejections of popular New Deal legislation. His success at gaining institutional acceptance for his judicial innovations depended in part on his sensitivity to the arguments against activism.

Judicial activism without controversy is difficult to accomplish. In the 1960s, the activism of the Warren Court generated so much controversy that many observers believed the court had suffered a devastating self-inflicted wound to its reputation and authority. The activism of Rose Bird, one of Traynor's successors as chief justice of the California Supreme Court, so inflamed the public that it resulted in her electoral ouster from office in 1986. Traynor's style of activism differed from that of the Warren and Bird Courts. He shared values that Earl Warren and Rose Bird championed, but unlike the Warren Court, he did not make broad statements of principle in his innovative opinions, and unlike the Bird Court, he avoided direct opposition to measures as popular and viscerally important as the death penalty. Although Traynor's advo-

---

[7]Leuchtenburg, *The Supreme Court Reborn,* 237–259.
[8]See Laura Kalman, *The Strange Career of Legal Liberalism* (New Haven, 1996).

cacy of activism stood out in the intellectual history of judging as extreme, his style of activism was designed to avert controversy. His scientistic approach helped him to avoid the appearance of deciding cases based on politically charged value judgments. He believed that he had a duty to reform laws that did not comport with his conception of the public interest, but the objective-sounding tone of his innovative opinions reflected his sensitivity to contemporary liberal fear of activism. In contrast with the activism of the Warren Court and the California Supreme Court under Chief Justice Rose Bird, Traynor's style of activism helped him to avoid a "self-inflicted wound" to the Court's prestige. Within the legal community, Traynor's innovative opinions often generated some criticism of his activism. However, his adroit articulation of the public interest made his reforms acceptable to other judges, even though his innovative opinions often dealt with controversial topics. Despite such controversy and despite the controversial nature of judicial activism itself, many of Traynor's activist opinions gained public acquiescence and widespread approval within the legal community.

CHAPTER ONE

The Foundations of Roger Traynor's Activist Jurisprudence

Oliver Wendell Holmes once said, "The life of the law has not been logic: it has been experience."[2] Roger Traynor's earliest intellectual experiences suggest why Traynor believed that judges should "descend to the everyday business of life to make . . . decisions."[3] Born in 1900, he grew up in Park City, Utah, surrounded by mountainous terrain he later compared to the path of a judge.[4] Park City was a mining town, and Traynor fondly remembered its color and diversity as part of his earliest education.

> [Park City] was much more than a park and much less than a city. . . . It re-sounded by day with the rumble of wagons laden with ore from the great mines and met evening with candlelight and coal oil lamps and here and there an electric light. It was not freer than any other place from the provincialism and prejudice and sudden gusts of crowd hysteria, but it managed to accommodate the heterogeneous speech and wants and beliefs of people who had come from all over the world to call it home. . . . [It] was a land of Bohunks and Micks and Krauts and Cousin Jacks. In these rude labels of identification that are part of our vivid speech there is nothing evil if they are free of vicious gloss, and I

---

[1]Roger Traynor, "La Rude Vita, La Dolce Guistizia; or Hard Cases Make Good Law," *University of Chicago Law Review* 29:223, 230 (1962).

[2]Oliver Wendell Holmes, *The Common Law* (Boston, 1963), 5.

[3]Traynor "La Rude Vita," 223, 230.

[4]Elizabeth Roth, "The Two Voices of Roger Traynor," *American Journal of Legal History,* Vol. 27(3): 269, 288 (1963).

1

should count it a loss if we were to become so self-consciously mannered as to
shut the windows of the parlor and the study to the language of the street, such
labels remain innocuous so long as we value diversity.[5]

Although Traynor described his upbringing in colorful terms, life in Park
City must have been difficult. Traynor's parents Felix and Elizabeth (O'Hagan)
Traynor emigrated from Hilltown, County Down in Northern Ireland.[6] His father
was a miner in Nevada and Utah until occupational disease forced him to quit
when Traynor was six. Traynor helped his father with a drayage business until
his father died several years later.[7] Although Traynor left Utah as a young man,
his upbringing in Park City made him attentive to the "language of the street"
throughout his career on the bench.

Traynor demonstrated an interest in practical policy questions early in his
academic career. He received a scholarship to attend the University of California, Berkeley, and after obtaining his bachelor's degree in 1923, he stayed on as
a graduate student in political science and then in law at Boalt Hall. Even as a
student he showed independence from law school conventions. Most American
law teachers were then firmly committed to the case study method originated by
Christopher Columbus Langdell, a proponent of the oracular theory of judging.
According to this theory, students could be taught to discern the enduring principles of the law through the study of judicial decisions.[8] Traynor appears always to have been skeptical of this theory. In his writings as a graduate student,
he examined legal questions from a policy perspective. Each of his five student
comments in the *California Law Review* dealt with practical, policy questions,
not questions of legal principle.[9] His political science Ph.D. dissertation ana-

---

[5]Roger Traynor, "Many Worlds Times You" (address at the University of Utah
commencement), (June 9, 1963).
[6]J. Edward Johnson, "Biography of Chief Justice Roger Traynor," *History of the
Supreme Court Justices of California,* Vol. 2 (San Francisco, 1966).
[7]*Ibid.*
[8]See generally Robert Stevens, *Law School's Legal Education in America from the
1800s to the 1900s* (Chapel Hill, 1983); and John H. Schlegel, *American Realism and
Empirical Social Science* (Chapel Hill, 1995).
[9]See Comment, "Adverse Possession: Personal Property: Tracking and Payment of
Taxes, *California Law Review* 14:218 (1926); Comment, "Inheritance Taxation: Tax Payable
at Domicile of Testator on Intangible Personalty in Another Jurisdiction, *California Law
Review* 14:225 (1926); Comment, "Taxation: Stock Issued by Reorganized Corporation as
Income," *California Law Review* 14:244 (1926); Comment, "Real Property: Landlord and
Tenant: The Rule in Dumpor's Case," *California Law Review* 14:328 (1926); and Comment,
"Damages: Date at Which Rate of Exchange Should be Applied," *California Law Review*
14:405 (1926).

lyzed the process for amending the United States Constitution.[10] It did not foreshadow his reformist tendencies on the bench. To the contrary, it criticized various contemporary reform proposals that advocated a less demanding amendment process. Based on his analysis of colonial experiences with charter amendments and the history of constitutional amendments, Traynor concluded that the provisions for amending the Constitution reflected the policies best suited to the needs of republican government.[11] His dissertation approached its topic pragmatically, scrutinizing the history of constitutional amendments to determine whether the amendment process accommodated contemporary political conditions and served contemporary political needs. Traynor critically examined the amendment process as a system of rules made coherent by a coherent system of policy objectives. He employed this pragmatic approach and systemic perspective throughout his career on the bench.

Traynor's law school experience at Berkeley was not exclusively in the Langdell tradition. It also exposed him to the ideas of the Legal Realists. He took constitutional law from Thomas Reed Powell, a visiting professor from Columbia. Powell was a proponent of Legal Realism, and his class fascinated Traynor.[12] Legal Realism at Columbia was inspiring the adoption of curricular changes oriented around the practical categorization of legal subjects and the use of nonlegal course materials. Boalt Hall, which had already established a reputation as a progressive law school, instituted changes that reflected these trends. It added courses such as criminology, which was cotaught by the Berkeley police chief. Boalt's shift away from pedagogical conventions sometimes sparked lively debate with the school. For instance, the appointment of Dr. Herman Adler, a psychologist, to teach criminal law, divided the faculty.[13] Traynor could not have avoided awareness of the changes in legal education initiated by the ideas of the Legal Realists.

Orrin Kip McMurray, who became dean in 1924, kept an open mind to the ideas of the Legal Realists. Although he opposed the trend toward opening the ranks of law school professors to nonlawyers, he disliked the conventional casestudy method.[14] Like many Boalt professors he embraced some politically unpopular causes. In 1925—in what became an important U.S. Supreme Court case—he opposed the prosecution of Oakland social worker Anita Whitney under the California criminal syndicalism act because he considered the law un-

---

[10] Roger Traynor, "The Amending of the United States Constitution, An Historical and Legal Analysis" (Ph.D. thesis, University of California, Berkeley, 1927).

[11] *Ibid.*, 205.

[12] Sandra Pearl Epstein, "Law at Berkeley: The History of Boalt Hall" (Ph.D. thesis, University of California, Berkeley), 146–47 (1979).

[13] *Ibid.*

[14] *Ibid.*

constitutional.[15] He also shared with the Legal Realists some basic assumptions about the law. In 1917 he wrote, "In theory the development of the law is the application of the rules of formal logic to fact and established principles found in legislation or judicial precedents. In reality it is the result of human factors of which the personalities of the judges are not the least important."[16]

Traynor's time as a student at Boalt Hall saw significant changes within the legal profession. During the late 1920s the movement to raise professional standards for California lawyers had gained several important victories. In the 1925–1926 academic year Boalt separated from the University of California undergraduate program.[17] The law school became a three-year program.[18] The California State Bar meanwhile became a self-governing body, devoted to the elevation of professional standards for lawyers.[19] Finally, a new standardized bar exam was instituted, leading to stricter, more uniform educational requirements for lawyers.[20]

Traynor joined the faculty at Boalt Hall in 1929, while McMurray was dean, and became close to faculty members Barbara Armstrong and Max Radin, both of whom were prominent in liberal causes. In 1928 Armstrong taught a course on the then-unusual topic of law and the problems of poverty, and during the New Deal she worked on Social Security legislation as a consultant to the Commission on Economic Security.[21] She and Traynor remained close even after Traynor ascended to the bench, and she exerted a strong influence over Traynor, particularly on questions involving the legal status of women. Radin had extensive contacts with the Democratic Party in California, and in 1935 he led a faculty effort to oppose anticommunist legislation. He clashed with another Boalt man, then-Alameda County District Attorney Earl Warren, over the case of a prominent union official convicted of murder in the famous Ramsey-King case.[22] This conflict not only affected Radin's later career, but Traynor's as well.

In August 1940, Governor Culbert Olson nominated Traynor to the Supreme Court after the State Qualifications Committee rejected Radin, the governor's previous nominee. The Qualifications Committee feared Radin's "radical

---

[15]*Ibid.,* 226. On the Whitney case in its historical context, see Stephen R. Rhode, "Criminal Syndicalism: The Repression of Free Speech in California," *Western Legal History* 3:309–40 (1990).

[16]As quoted in Epstein, *op. cit.,* 145.

[17]*Ibid.,* 170–71.

[18]*Ibid.*

[19]*Ibid.*

[20]*Ibid.*

[21]*Ibid.,* 239, 193.

[22]*Ibid.,* 224–25.

tendencies."[23] Then-Attorney General Earl Warren was one of two members of the Qualifications Commission to vote against Radin.[24] Although Radin's chance to sit on the state Supreme Court faded after the ugly confirmation fight, Radin was not jealous of Traynor's success. To the contrary, when Governor Olson called Radin to ask his advice on a substitute nominee, Radin immediately recommended Traynor.[25] Traynor was an uncontroversial choice for the state Supreme Court. Although he lacked judicial experience, he also lacked unattractive political affiliations. Radin, however, could assure his well-placed Democratic friends of Traynor's sympathies.

Traynor already had become well known in California legal circles as the state's leading tax expert when Governor Olson nominated him to the California Supreme Court.[26] He taught one of the first tax classes at Boalt Hall in 1929,[27] and he served at different times as counsel to the Tax Research Bureau, consultant to the State Board of Equalization, and deputy attorney general in the tax division.[28] When California restructured its revenue system in the wake of the Depression, Traynor was the chief architect of the new design.[29] Before joining the bench he wrote or helped to write the laws that formed the foundation of California's tax system: the Bank and Corporations Tax Act, the Retail Sales Tax Act, the Motor Vehicle Transportation License Tax Act, the Personal Income Tax Act, the Use Tax Act, the Corporate Income Tax Act, the Private Car Tax Act, and the Use Fuel Tax Act.[30] His role in revamping the state's tax laws demanded a circumspect analytical approach, which, like many of his later decisions as a judge, advanced a system of rules based on public policy preferences. Traynor's experiences critiquing and reforming the tax code helped him establish a systemic approach toward legal reform that echoed through his judicial decisions.

Traynor's career on the California Supreme Court from 1940 to 1970 spanned 30 years of explosive social change in California. During his tenure on the bench, the population of California tripled, and the state became much more urban. Employment patterns changed, dramatically impacting family life and

[23] *Los Angeles Times,* August 8, 1940.

[24] *Bakersfield Californian,* August 3, 1940.

[25] Professor Stephan Riesenfeld, who happened to be in Radin's office when the governor called, reported this conversation to me when I interviewed him on September 29, 1993.

[26] Interview with Professor Adrian Kragen by Ben Field, August 15, 1997.

[27] Interview with Professor Richard Jennings by Ben Field, August 15, 1997. Jennings was one of Traynor's students.

[28] Roth, "The Two Voices of Roger Traynor," 295.

[29] James Sabine, "Taxation: A Delicate, Planned Arrangement of Cargo," *California Law Review* 53:174, 174 (1965).

[30] *Ibid.*

gender roles. The growing demand for new, mass-marketed products emerged as a dominant characteristic of middle-class economic life. World War II, the Cold War, and domestic consumerism changed the dynamics of race relations. Attitudes about the role of government in the lives of individuals changed as well. Ensuring an increased level of economic security for individuals became a widely accepted objective of government. Simultaneously, there arose antipathy toward government infringements on individual rights.

Traynor's understanding of the social, economic, and political events of the post-New Deal Era corresponded with a cohesive set of concerns, values, prejudices, and sympathies that formed his ideological lens. He believed that judge-made law at its best reflected a "value judgment as to what the law ought to be," and his thinking frequently reflected the influence of three distinct, but intertwined ideological influences: philosophical Pragmatism, Legal Realism, and the scholarly debate surrounding it, and contemporary liberalism.[31]

The Pervasive Influence of Pragmatism

It has often been pointed out that Pragmatism had a pervasive influence on legal scholars and judges in the first decades of the century. Pragmatism has been characterized as a revolt against the formalism of nineteenth-century thinking. Like many contemporary legal thinkers influenced by Pragmatism, Traynor rejected the jurisprudential conventions of the nineteenth century. He denied that the law existed as a set of immutable principles that could be discovered through careful examination of case law.

Traynor's activism reflected his Pragmatic notion of the nature of the law. He believed the common law was the result of bringing judicial experience to bear on the facts of legal disputes. This conception of the law paralleled the thinking of William James and John Dewey. James believed that law—and truth—were man-made, the results of inquiries into the circumstances of life.[32] He posited that truth was not an "inert static relation" between an idea and reality, but an attribute gained by an idea that is validated by reality.[33] Dewey expressed similar views. "A moral law, like a law in physics, is not something to swear by and stick to at all hazards," he wrote.[34] Like James and Dewey, Traynor did not think of the law as existing in a fixed, immutable relationship

---

[31]Traynor, "La Rude Vita," 223.

[32]William James, *Pragmatism* (Indianapolis, 1981), 109–10.

[33]*Ibid.*, 92.

[34]John Dewey, *The Quest for Certainty,* as quoted in James Kloppenberg, *Uncertain Victory: Social Democracy and Progressivism in European and American Thought, 1870–1920* (New York, 1986), 135.

between principles and the facts of legal cases. He believed instead that the law ought to resonate with the circumstances of life.

The transitory nature of the relationship between legal rules and the circumstances of life created the need for law reform. As William James wrote in *Pragmatism,* "we have to live to-day by what truth we can get to-day, and be ready to-morrow to call it falsehood."[35] In *People v. Cahan,* Traynor would overrule a precedent that he himself had established because he believed changed circumstances justified the change in the law. (See chapter 4, below.) "The composite ideal of the professors," he once wrote,

> is a judge who, after marshalling an impressive array of relevant facts, can write an opinion that gives promise of more than a three-year lease on life by accurately anticipating the near future, who respects established folk patterns by not anticipating the too distant future, and who walks a tightrope of logic to the satisfaction of a team of collective thinkers as well as to the plaudits of the philosophers.[36]

Traynor saw the role of the judge as fundamentally reactive: "[W]ell tempered judges will do the best they can . . . to stabilize the explosive forces of the day," he wrote.[37] It was societal change and not judges themselves that initiated change. Judges provided an element of certainty in an uncertain, sometimes irrational world.

The Pragmatic notion of the impermanence of law was a foundational assumption of Traynor's jurisprudence. It justified the effort to search out and eliminate legal rules that Traynor believed no longer served their purpose. Traynor did not seek to make permanent the legal reforms he initiated. To the contrary, he expected his judicial decisions to stand only as long as they remained functional. "The great strength of the common law," he wrote, "has been its reconciliation of . . . stability with a continuing evolution that has enabled it to respond sooner or later to the recurring reminder that there is nothing forever . . . under the sun."[38] Traynor believed the common law ought to be a set of workable rules that met society's needs. "The demolition of obsolete theories makes the judge's task harder, as he works his way out of the wreckage," Traynor wrote, "but it leaves him free to weigh competing policies without pre-

---

[35]James, *Pragmatism,* 100.

[36]Roger Traynor, "No Magic Words Could Do It Justice," *California Law Review* 49:615, 625 (1961).

[37]*Ibid.,* at 124.

[38]Roger Traynor, "Stare Decisis versus Social Change" (dedication of new law building, Duke University, April 26–27, 1963, Traynor Papers).

conceptions that purport to compel the decision, but in fact do not."[39] Like the Pragmatists, Traynor sought to avoid dogma. His opinions lacked a tone of moral outrage even when he struck down laws he considered unjust. He justified his innovative decisions on the basis of practical considerations instead of broad principles that tended to ossify.

Like the Pragmatist philosophers, Traynor embraced an ideal of action.[40] The law was an instrument of action for him, just as ideas were instruments of action for John Dewey. In Traynor's opinion, judges did not eliminate outdated precedent frequently or quickly enough. "The danger," he wrote, "is not that they [judges] will exceed their power, but that they will fall short of their obligation."[41] Traynor believed that deciding some cases required a process of policy analysis, guided by reason and the most accurate, most current societal data available. The prospect of such judicial policy analysis caused great anxiety among other legal scholars and jurists of Traynor's day. They found themselves torn between their skepticism about legal precedent and their fear of the subjectivity of judicial decisions in the absence of guiding precedents. Traynor's confidence in judicial policy analysis derived from his faith in the rationality of judges. Judges kept "the inevitable evolution of the law on a rational course."[42] Again, Traynor's conception of judicial lawmaking paralleled the Pragmatic conception of truth. Truth was "an idea that will carry us prosperously from any one part of our experience to any other part," William James wrote, "linking things satisfactorily, working securely simplifying, saving labor; [something] is true for just so much, true in so far forth, true instrumentally."[43] Like truth, the law was for Traynor a product of purposeful human inquiry.

Traynor believed that legal reform should be humanistic in the Pragmatic sense; the law was good or bad to the extent that it served human needs. The operation of laws in society tested their functionality. John Dewey wrote, a moral law "is a formula . . . [whose] soundness and pertinence are tested by what happens when it is acted upon."[44] Like Dewey and James, Traynor understood the law to operate within a societal context.

Novel legal problems need not take him (the judge) by storm if he makes a little advanced, uncloistered inquiry into what people most want out of their

---

[39]Roger Traynor, "Law and Social Change in a Democratic Society," *University of Illinois Law Forum* (1956), 230.

[40]For a discussion of the pragmatic ideal of action see David Hollinger, "The Problem of Pragmatism in American History," *Journal of American History,* Vol. LXVII, No. 1 (June 1980): 88, 105.

[41]Traynor, "No Magic Words Could Do It Justice," 615, 620.

[42]Traynor, "The Limits of Judicial Creativity," 1, 7.

[43]As quoted in Hollinger, "The Problem of Pragmatism," 88, 97.

[44]Dewey, *The Quest for Certainty* as quoted in Kloppenberg, *Uncertain Victory,* 135.

lives and how they wish to live with one another. It is from the stuff of their relationships with one another and with the state that the common law develops.[45]

For Traynor, the functionality of the law depended on its resonance with community needs.

Traynor's conception of community needs was consensualist. He believed that, despite their diversity, Americans were fundamentally unified; he believed that they shared basic interests regardless of race, gender, or class and that judges could identify those interests. He often justified his innovative decisions on the grounds that they served the "public interest." Without this confidence in the unity of the community and the commonality of its interests he could not have thought such a "public interest" existed, much less that judges would be able to ascertain the "public interest" through the analysis of societal data.

In keeping with his belief that a fundamental objective of the law was to meet societal demands, Traynor insisted that judges ought to look beyond the facts given in briefs and consider "legislative facts or what we might call environmental data."[46] Indeed, the law would have to struggle to keep pace with the sciences, including the social sciences. "[T]here is increasing concern," Traynor wrote, "that an evolution of sorts in the law may no longer be good enough to match the revolutionary changes that science and the attendant revolution of rising expectations in the world are making on our lives."[47] Traynor feared that if judges did not take into account the dramatic changes occurring in society the common law would atrophy and perhaps become a complete anachronism.

Traynor's method of judging involved a process of inquiry and social verification that paralleled the Pragmatists' concept of scientific method.[48] William James argued that:

> We must find a theory that will work and that means something extremely difficult; for our theory must mediate between all previous truths and certain new experiences. It must derange common sense and previous belief as little as possible, and it must lead to some sensible terminus or other that can be verified exactly.[49]

---

[45] Traynor, "Better Days in Court," 109, 109.

[46] Traynor, "No Magic Words," 615, 627.

[47] *Ibid.,* 623.

[48] For a discussion of the pragmatic theory of scientific inquiry in the context of Oliver Wendell Holmes's jurisprudence see Morton White, *Social Thought in America: The Revolt against Formalism* (Boston, 1957), 208.

[49] As quoted in Morton White, *Science and Sentiment in America: Philosophical Thought from Jonathan Edwards to John Dewey* (Boston, 1972), 209.

According to the Pragmatists, the scientific method of inquiry could produce functional truths, propositions that served some useful purpose. Dewey argued that knowledge was valid only to the extent that the scientific method of inquiry confirmed it.[50] Similarly, Traynor asserted that the final test of a judge's written opinion was whether it worked for the people who used it. "Never forget," he wrote, "that his [the judge's] explanation must persuade his colleagues, make sense to the bar, pass muster with the scholars, and if possible allay the suspicion of any man in the street who regards knowledge of the law as no excuse for making it."[51] Judges could produce functional law through policy analysis, much as scientists could produce scientific truth through inquiry.

According to Traynor, the reaction of the legal community to the reasoning and factual support set forth in a judicial opinion provided a form of quality assurance.

> The disinterestedness of the creative decision is further assured by the judge's arduous articulation of the reasons that compelled the formulation of an original solution and by the full disclosure in his opinion of all aspects of the problem and of the data pertinent to its solution. Thereafter the opinion must pass muster with scholars and practitioners on the alert to note any misunderstanding of the problem at hand.[52]

The process of pragmatic verification of the functionality of judicial decisions occurred through the scrutiny of the legal community. Although the judiciary lacked any institutional means of gathering societal data, Traynor believed the information necessary for the process of verification would become known to judges. The inherent elitism of this approach did not trouble Traynor. Such was his faith in the abilities of judges.

Traynor's theory of judging glossed over conceptual difficulties with his idea of functionality. He ignored the possibility of competing visions of functionality based on competing societal values. Scholars and legal practitioners would assent to good judicial policy because the light of reason would enable them to recognize its functionality. Traynor's thinking on this point was driven by his consensualist view of public interest and his belief in the possibility of objectivity in human judgment. Unlike William James, who explained that man was not capable of objectivity,[53] Traynor insisted that reason could inform judgment without the intervention of other internal influences. Traynor's belief

---

[50]White, *Science and Sentiment in America,* 273.

[51]Traynor, "Badlands in an Appellate Judge's Realm," 157, 166.

[52]Roger Traynor, "Comment" on Justice Charles Breitel's "The Courts and Law Making" in Monrad G. Paulsen, ed., *Legal Institutions Today and Tomorrow* (New York, 1959), 52.

[53]See White, *Science and Sentiment in America,* 195.

in the power of reason and scientific policy analysis was an article of faith for him, and it gave his theory of judging a simplistic quality.

Roger Traynor's Response to Legal Realism

The idea of judicial creativity caused great anxiety among legal scholars and jurists during the first half of the twentieth century. Building on the judicial philosophy of Oliver Wendell Holmes, Legal Realism emerged in the 1920s and thirties as a disparate school of jurisprudence devoted to exploring the uncertainty of judicial lawmaking. Traynor's career on the California Supreme Court coincided with widespread controversy among the Realists and other contemporary legal scholars about the arbitrariness of judicial decisions. Although Traynor differed with the Legal Realists on some important jurisprudential points, they helped prepare the way for Traynor's approach toward judging. The Legal Realist critique of what has been called Formalism undermined the traditional justifications for judicial decision making and offered a new conception of the role of judges.

Legal Realism was a somewhat loosely defined school of thought, identified with a group of law professors—mostly from Columbia and Yale Law Schools—including Karl Llewellyn, Thurman Arnold, Felix Cohen, Fred Rodell, Jerome Frank, Herman Oliphant, and Max Radin. Laura Kalman has defined Legal Realism as functionalism in a legal context, that is an attempt to understand law in terms of its social and economic context, as opposed to conceptualism, an attempt to reduce law to a set of stable principles.[54] Traynor's approach toward judging embraced this legal functionalism. He shared with the Legal Realists a pragmatic distaste for abstraction, a preference for reform, and an insistence on the need to take into account the societal effects of the law.

Wilfred Rumble, Jr., has characterized Legal Realism as devoted to certain questions about judicial decision making, the role of rules and judicial objectivity.[55] Legal Realists discredited formalism by showing the limited influence of rules on judicial decisions and the substantial influence of extralegal factors. The writings of those most commonly associated with Legal Realism support Rumble's characterization. Karl Llewellyn's 1931 article "Some Realism about Realism—Responding to Dean Pound" argued that Realism was a movement that focused attention on the role of law in society. According to Llewellyn, Legal Realists shared certain points of departure. They believed that legal change occurred through judicial innovation, they advocated the use of law as a means to

---

[54]Laura Kalman, *Legal Realism at Yale 1927–1960* (New Haven, 1986).

[55]Wilfred Rumble, Jr., *American Legal Realism: Skepticism, Reform and Judicial Process* (Ithaca, New York, 1969).

achieve socially desirable ends, and they emphasized the pressures placed on the legal system by rapid social change.

Traynor immersed himself in the scholarly debate over the mysteries of judging. He knew and read the work of Realist scholars, such as Jerome Frank, Karl Llewellyn, and Max Radin. He even wrote an essay responding to Frank's influential argument in *Courts on Trial* regarding fact skepticism and rule skepticism.[56] He also cited Llewellyn's Realist classic *The Common Law Tradition* in several law review articles.[57] Frank endorsed Traynor's nomination to the California Supreme Court, though Traynor was a political unknown at the time.[58] However, Traynor's closest relationship was with Max Radin, who served as dean of the Boalt Hall Law School while Traynor was a professor there, and, as mentioned earlier, recommended Traynor for the Court when his own nomination foundered.

Traynor agreed with the Realists on certain fundamental propositions about the nature of judging. He and the Realists rejected the proposition that law was composed of fixed principles. Citing Radin's *The Theory of Judicial Decision,* Traynor argued that immutable principles of law might rely on assumptions that could not withstand the test of time.[59] Traynor agreed with the Legal Realists that judges made law, and that, when they did so, extralegal factors often influenced their decisions. He did not, however, share the anxiety of many of the Legal Realists over the absence of fixed legal principles or their cynicism about the legitimacy of judge-made law. Traynor's conviction that judges made the law conflicted with the traditional role of the judge. If Oliver Wendell Holmes, the philosophical progenitor of Realism, was correct that law reflected "the felt necessities of the time, the prevalent moral and political theories, intuitions of public policy, avowed or unconscious, even the prejudices which judges share with their fellow men," judicial decisions had to find a new jurisprudential justification.[60] But while many of the Realists brooded over the arbitrariness of judicial decisions, Traynor candidly encouraged judicial innovation.

Llewellyn and other Legal Realists distinguished the unconscious processes that determined judicial decisions from the process of rationalizing those decisions in the form of a written opinion. Much Legal Realist scholarship was devoted to the development of behavioral theories capable of explaining and even

---

[56]Roger Traynor, "Fact Skepticism and the Judicial Process," *University of Pennsylvania Law Review* 106:635 (1958).

[57]See Traynor, "Badlands in an Appellate Judge's Realm," 157; Traynor, "No Magic Words," 615.

[58]Johnson, *History of the Supreme Court Justices of California,* Vol. 2, "Biography of Chief Justice Roger Traynor."

[59]Traynor, "Badlands in an Appellate Judge's Realm," 157, 161.

[60]Holmes, *The Common Law,* 5.

predicting judicial opinions. With the important exception of Jerome Frank, who had little hope that such studies would make judge-made law more predictable, the Legal Realists attempted to identify the process of judicial decision making through the study of judicial behavior.

The Legal Realists disagreed among themselves considerably about the factors that caused and inhibited judicial innovation. However, as Bruce Ackerman has pointed out, they all aspired to protect the existing common law system from the threat of structural change:

> In its time Legal Realism was the legal profession's *enfant terrible*—debunking cherished legal myths. But in hindsight it seems profoundly conservative. Rather than transforming traditional legal discourse, the Realist critique allowed the profession to survive the New Deal without restructuring its basic conceptual framework. . . . Realism argued for a new, more sensitive common law based on gradual accretion of decisions from distinct factual situations versus the alternative, which demanded theoretical reconciliation with the common law and legislative and bureaucratic practices. Realism protected the ideal of the common law even though the common law was founded on *laissez faire* theory.[61]

The Legal Realists carefully scrutinized the concept of judge as policymaker, and it caused them great anxiety. Most Legal Realists were skeptical about the prospects for judicial objectivity and predictability. They feared naked judicial creativity might erode legal certainty—an essential attribute of the common law—and clash with democratic theory. Judging, when stripped of its claim to the legitimacy of time-honored rules, would succumb to the prejudices of judges. As a result, the law would become unpredictable and inconsistent; judicial rulings liberated from precedent would be unruly. The Legal Realists' behavioral theories of judging were an attempt to provide a new source of predictability.[62]

Unlike the Legal Realists, Traynor did not fear the prospect of judicial creativity. He anticipated Ackerman's argument that judges played a conservative role in the sense that their creativity helped to preserve the common law in the face of social change. He insisted that careful judicial innovation would be an improvement over slavish adherence to legal rules he considered obsolete. The alternative to innovative judicial lawmaking frightened Traynor. If judges failed to modernize the law, the law as an institution might lose its legitimacy and col-

---

[61]Bruce Ackerman, *Reconstructing American Law* (Cambridge, Massachusetts, 1984).

[62]See Edward Purcell, Jr., "American Jurisprudence between the Wars: Legal Realism and the Crisis of Democratic Theory," in Lawrence Friedman and Harry Scheiber, eds., *American Law and the Constitutional Order: Historical Perspectives* (Cambridge, Massachusetts, 1988), 359.

lapse under the weight of changing social conditions. The transformation of the living law into an anachronism might even prepare the way for antidemocratic forces. Traynor's decisions on criminal procedure, in particular, exhibit the fear that "[I]f he [the judge] tends it [the law] badly or merely passively, it can develop weaknesses or disorders or, worse still, frightening powers."[63] For Traynor, the threat to democracy came not from judicial decision making, but from the aversion to it.

While Traynor expressed fear that judicial passivity could undermine democratic values, other legal scholars during the mid and late 1930s made the opposite argument. They attacked Legal Realism, arguing that it promoted moral relativism by asserting the essential and inescapable subjectivity of judicial decision making. Judge Learned Hand contended that the principles of Realist jurisprudence were "that a judge should not regard the law; that this has never really been done in the past, and that to attempt to do it is an illusion."[64] As World War II approached, criticism of Legal Realism became increasingly severe. According to Edward Purcell, Jr., "The American legal profession became the forum for one of the most bitter and sustained intellectual debates in the nation's history."[65] Legal Realism, its critics claimed, undermined democracy by denying any connection between law and morality and by defining law in terms of coercive government action. Several of the Legal Realists recanted some of their more provocative opinions in the face of such harsh criticism.

Traynor insisted that judges would not abuse their power to innovate because caution typified the professional culture of the bench. Their freedom from political influence, their detachment from adversarial interests, and their tradition of public service insulated them from bias.[66] "The disinterestedness of the creative decision," Traynor wrote, "is further assured by the judge's arduous articulation of the reasons that compel the formulation of an original solution and by the full disclosure in his opinion of all aspects of the problem and of the data pertinent to its solution."[67] The pragmatic process of verification by scholars and practitioners would limit the impact of any wrongheaded judicial innovations.

Traynor believed that the power of judicial creativity emanated from the judge's ability to persuade lawyers to accept and other judges to follow innovative opinions. Because the professional ethos of the bench discouraged individuality, judges would innovate cautiously and only when they believed their opinions would gain support in the legal community. Traynor's confidence in the

---

[63]Traynor, "Better Days in Court," 109, 123.

[64]As quoted in White, *The American Judicial Tradition,* 268.

[65]Purcell, "American Jurisprudence between the Wars," 359, 359.

[66]Traynor, "Badlands in an Appellate Judge's Realm," 157, 167.

[67]Traynor, "Comment" on Justice Charles Breitel's "The Courts and Lawmaking," 52.

innate caution of the judiciary was at the heart of his argument for judicial creativity. However, his justification for judicial activism went beyond this assumption about the professional culture of the bench and delved into the difficult
theoretical questions that concerned the Legal Realists. Traynor believed that
judges could objectively consider the facts and competing legal policies involved in a case. They were "uniquely situated to articulate timely rules of reason . . . as independent and analytically objective as that of the legal scholars,"
he wrote.[68] He believed that judges could rise above their conditioning.

He (the judge) knows well enough that he must severely discount his own
predilections, of however high grade he regards them, which is to say that he
must bring to his intellectual labors a cleansing doubt of his omniscience, indeed
even of his perception.[69]

Like the Pragmatist philosophers, the Legal Realists denied that people
could view the world with objectivity. The Legal Realists devoted themselves to
the exploration of judicial behavior because they believed that judicial decisions
reflected deep-seated prejudices, desires, and aversions. Traynor's insistence on
the possibility of objectively reasoned judgment constituted the most significant
theoretical difference between Traynor's thinking and that of the Legal Realists.

Traynor attempted to answer concerns raised by the Realists about judicial
subjectivity. Legal Realists argued that judicial decisions were result-oriented in
that judges reasoned backwards from results chosen on the basis of their subjec-
tive values.[70] They saw judicial rationality, expressed through the language of
decisions, as a facade. Traynor disagreed, arguing that judges could reason their
way to "the good" result.[71]

He [the judge] comes to realize how essential it is . . . that he be intellectually
interested in a rational outcome . . . he can strive to deepen his inquiry and his
reflection enough to arrive at last at a value judgment as to what the law ought
to be and spell out why. In the course of doing so he channels his interest in a
rational outcome into an interest in a particular result. In that limited sense he
becomes result-oriented.[72]

Traynor wrote that the act of judging was not the rationalization of a pre-
conceived result, but the willful and systematic pursuit of a rational result.[73]
However, he also admitted that the judge's "rational outcome" depended on a

---

[68]Traynor, "Badlands in an Appellate Judge's Realm," 157, 167.

[69]Traynor, "La Rude Vita," 223, 234.

[70]Karl Llewellyn, "Realism in Jurisprudence—the Next Step," *Columbia Law Review*
30:431, 444 (1930); White, *The American Judicial Tradition,* 273.

[71]Traynor, "La Rude Vita," 223, 235.

[72]*Ibid.,* 234.

[73]*Ibid.,* 235.

"value judgment." His writings failed to explain how this "value judgment" could be "rational" or "analytically objective." He left unresolved the conceptual tension between values and reason, providing little basis for his faith in judicial objectivity other than his confidence in the professional ethos of judicial restraint.

Traynor's sanguine assessment of judicial objectivity and rationality supported his view that the judiciary could be held responsible for the health of the law. The judge's "quality control" function in the legal process demanded that as soon as a precedent became outdated, the judge should eliminate it.[74] Traynor never mourned the death of a precedent he considered outdated. A "bad precedent is doubly evil," he insisted, "because it has not only wrought hardship but threatens to continue wreaking it."[75] Traynor not only accepted the idea of the judge as lawmaker, he explicitly encouraged judges to take a creative part in shaping the law. The stability of the law depended not on its permanence, but on its flexibility. While Realist scholars doubted that judges could transcend their prejudices, Traynor not only believed they could, but asserted that the health of the law depended on their willingness to innovate.

Traynor and the Ideological Environment of the Post-New Deal Era

Traynor was not politically active, and he shared his political views freely only with his close friends. Donald Barrett, the senior staff attorney at the California Supreme Court and a close friend of Traynor's, referred to Traynor as a "loyal Democrat."[76] Former Traynor clerk Herma Hill Kay described him as "progressive."[77] Barrett remembered Traynor's jubilation when Harry Truman was elected president. When Douglas MacArthur paraded through San Francisco after President Harry Truman fired him, Traynor refused to get up from his desk to watch, even though the parade went directly under his office window. After making a remark he thought might have offended any Republicans who might be present in his office to watch the parade he asked a clerk whether he was a Democrat. When the clerk answered affirmatively, Traynor is said to have responded, "Well, most intelligent people are."[78] These expressions of political sympathies were, however, rare.

---

[74] *Ibid.*, 229.

[75] *Ibid.*, 231.

[76] Interview with Don Barrett by Ben Field, May 24, 1997.

[77] Interview with Dean Herma Hill Kay by Ben Field, August 15, 1997.

[78] Interview with Don Barrett by Ben Field, May 24, 1997.

Partisanship affected the Court insofar as the Democratic appointees to the Court frequently voted the same way. Governor Olson, the only Democratic governor from 1900–1958, appointed four judges during his 1938–1942 term in office. According to Barrett they dominated the Court.[79] As noted earlier, from 1945 to 1956, during what Barrett called the "Long Court," the Court's composition did not change.[80] It was during that period that the Court, led by Traynor and Chief Justice Phil Gibson, handed down many of their most innovative decisions.

Traynor put into practice his judicial philosophy of "uncloistered inquiry." His innovative opinions explicitly took into account the societal context in which they occurred. They often referred to sources of "environmental data" outside the text of the law.[81] Traynor's values, prejudices, historical associations, and sentimental commitments affected his assessment of the "environmental data." In this sense, Traynor viewed cases before the Court through an ideological lens. The issues Traynor raised in his innovative opinions, the concerns he expressed, the types of arguments he articulated, and the language he used revealed the contours of his ideological lens. His opinions in cases involving racial discrimination, particularly the antimiscegenation case of *Perez v. Sharp*, showed his predisposition toward racial egalitarianism and the impact of the war against fascism on his thinking.[82] His precedent-breaking opinion in the divorce case of *DeBurgh v. DeBurgh* demonstrated his belief in gender equality and his awareness of changes in the institution of the family and the role of women.[83] Themes of cold war politics—the threat of domestic communism and the countervailing threat of an extreme reaction to it—echoed through his groundbreaking decision in *People v. Cahan* and his other writings on police investigative methods.[84] The rise of mass marketing and mass consumption during Traynor's tenure on the bench influenced his thinking in product liability cases; his innovative opinions in *Escola v. Coca Cola* and *Greenman v. Yuba Power Products* revealed his commitment to consumer protection as a matter of public interest.[85] Where Traynor departed from precedent his "value judgment as to what the law ought to be" manifested his assessment of the societal context of his decision.[86]

---

[79] *Ibid.*

[80] *Ibid.*

[81] Roger Traynor, "No Magic Words," 615, 627.

[82] Perez v. Sharp, 32 Cal.2d 711 (1948).

[83] DeBurgh v. DeBurgh, 39 Cal.2d 858 (1952).

[84] People v. Cahan, 44 Cal.2d 434 (1955).

[85] Escola v. Coca Cola, 24 Cal.2d 453 (1944); Greenman v. Yuba Power Products, 59 Cal.2d 57 (1963).

[86] Traynor, "La Rude Vita," 223, 234.

Traynor's value judgments in his innovative decisions, considered together, reflected a cohesive conception of the public interest. He believed the common weal required legal reforms that advanced individual liberties, and he associated individual liberty with race and gender equality. He was more likely than other judges to favor groups the law traditionally treated as inferior—racial minorities and women. He tended to be less tolerant than other contemporary judges of government intrusions into the lives of individuals. He was more likely than other judges to favor consumers over more powerful economic interests. Traynor's conception of public interest shared various attributes with contemporary liberal thought. His concern for the powerless, his tendency toward social egalitarianism, his fear of the "police state," and his proconsumer policy orientation resonated with contemporary liberalism, which was a dominant feature of the ideological environment during his tenure on the bench. His practical, policy-oriented approach toward judicial innovation reflected great confidence in the prospects for social progress through scientific policymaking. He unabashedly articulated policy-based justifications for legal reform, giving clear indications of his conception of the public interest and the values that shaped it.

CHAPTER TWO

Perez v. Sharp: Racial Assimilation and Judicial Lawmaking

Interracial sex and interracial marriage occupy a place at the emotional center of race relations. In *An American Dilemma,* his 1944 landmark study of black-white relations in the United States, Gunnar Myrdal observed that white fear of racial amalgamation formed the basis of the whole system of racial segregation and discrimination. "Every single measure [of segregation] is defended as necessary to block 'social equality,' which in its turn is held necessary to prevent 'intermarriage,'" he wrote. "Sex becomes in this popular theory the principle around which the whole structure of segregation of the Negroes—down to disfranchisement and denial of equal opportunities on the labor market—is organized."[1] The significance to whites of each measure of segregation depended on its importance as a means of upholding the ban on interracial marriage.

> In this rank order, (1) the ban on intermarriage and other sex relations involving white women and colored men takes precedence before everything else. It is the end for which the other restrictions are arranged as means. Thereafter follow: (2) all sorts of taboos and etiquettes in personal contacts; (3) segregation in schools and churches; (4) segregation in hotels, restaurants, and theaters, and other public places where people meet socially; (5) segregation in public con-

---

[1]Gunnar Myrdal, *An American Dilemma: The Negro Problem and Modern Democracy* (New York, 1944), 587.

19

veyances; (6) discrimination in public services; and finally, inequality in (7) politics, (8) justice and (9) breadwinning and relief.[2]

Myrdal's observations echoed through post-World War II commentary on interracial marriage. A writer in the 1949 *Stanford Law Review* observed that antimiscegenation statutes "lie at the foundation of the hierarchy of race prejudice."[3] Several commentators on school desegregation drew the connection between the integration of schools and increased prospects for interracial marriages.[4] Laws proscribing interracial marriage reflected widespread, deep-seated beliefs about race and the propriety of racial mixing.

Miscegenation has always been a political concept. Copperhead pamphleteers, David Croly and George Wakeman, invented the word miscegenation in 1864. It came from the Latin miscere—mix—and genus—race.[5] Croly and Wakeman first used the word in their pamphlet, "Miscegenation: The Theory of the Blending of the Races," charging that Civil War era Republicans intended to institute a plan of forced racial intermarriage.[6] The threat of race mixing generated visceral responses then, and it continued to do so in Roger Traynor's time.

Twentieth-century defenders of antimiscegenation statutes invariably claimed scientific support for their position. However, by the 1930s many reputable scientists and social scientists had discarded the assumptions that justified antimiscegenation statutes. World War II made those assumptions even more difficult to defend; the parallels between Nazi race dogma and racism in the United States made racial discrimination appear manifestly incongruous with American ideals.

Changes in the ideological climate surrounding race relations in the United States after World War II gradually began to produce a reevaluation of domestic racism. However, when the case of *Perez v. Sharp* came before the California Supreme Court in 1947, there was no political pressure on the Court to strike down California's antimiscegenation statute. No grass roots civil rights movement agitated against the law. No civil rights organization joined the fight against the statute. Although the National Association for the Advancement of Colored People had chapters in both Los Angeles and San Francisco, neither chapter played a role in the litigation. No civil rights organization filed a "friend of the court brief" in opposition to the law. Several commentators have noted that civil rights organizations and minority communities generally cared far less

---

[2]*Ibid.*, 587–88.
[3]"Statutory Bar on Interracial Marriage Invalidated by the 14th Amendment," *Stanford Law Review* 1:289, 297 (1949).
[4]See Robert J. Sickels, *Race, Marriage and the Law* (Albuquerque, 1972), 40.
[5]Sickels, *Race, Marriage and the Law,* footnote 2, page 1.
[6]Paul Spikard, *Mixed Blood: Intermarriage and Ethnic Identity in 20th Century America* (Madison, 1989), 283.

about antimiscegenation statutes than discrimination in employment and education.[7]

Public sentiment was strongly opposed to miscegenation when the Court invalidated the state's antimiscegenation statute in *Perez*. Although the percentage of blacks that married nonblacks in the United States reached no higher than one percent from 1865 through 1970, the fear of interracial mixing was widespread among whites.[8] Black-white couples had difficulty obtaining marriage licenses, finding ministers who would marry them, and finding places to live after they got married.[9] A 1958 Gallup poll showed that 92 percent of western whites opposed miscegenation.[10] Forty-eight percent of the adults surveyed in a 1965 Gallup poll approved of criminal antimiscegenation laws, 46 percent disapproved, and six percent had no opinion.[11] Seventy-two percent of the adults surveyed in a 1968 Gallup poll disapproved of marriage between whites and people of color, 20 percent approved, and eight percent had no opinion.[12] Although polling data on racial attitudes in 1947 is lacking, it is safe to assume that attitudes about interracial marriage had not become less tolerant between 1947 and the mid-1960s. If anything, those attitudes had become more tolerant. Disapproval of interracial marriage was at least as widespread at the time *Perez* reached the Court as it was in 1958 and 1965.

The fear of interracial mixing revealed itself in a few highly publicized incidents of the 1930s, forties, and fifties. The infamous Scottsboro case in 1931[13]

---

[7]See Myrdal, *An American Dilemma,* 56–57. Sickels, citing Myrdal, makes the same point: "From the point of view of the white man . . . intermarriage and sexual relations between black men and white women were the highest concern, followed in importance by social intercourse, segregation in schools and other facilities, political disfranchisement, discrimination in court and by police and financial discrimination in employment and welfare. To the black man . . . job and business opportunity head the list, with intermarriage at the very bottom. What is most likely to arouse white racist ire . . . is least likely to be championed by Negro civil rights organizations." Also, if this is so, it is probably not accidental that the Loving's case was fought through the appellate courts not by the NAACP but by the ACLU, a largely white organization of liberals. Sickels, *Race, Marriage and the Law,* 87.

[8]Joel Williamson, *The New People: Miscegenation and Mulattoes in the United States* (New York, 1980), 188.

[9]Spikard, *Mixed Blood,* 292.

[10]*Ibid.*

[11]Sickels, *Race, Marriage and the Law,* 42.

[12]*Ibid.*

[13]The case involved rape charges fabricated by two young, white women against nine young black men in Alabama. A rural, all white jury convicted all nine men, and the men were sentenced to death. The Supreme Court ultimately overturned the verdict in *Powell v. Alabama.*

and the murder 24 years later of Emmett Till in Mississippi[14] illustrated the visceral response of racist whites to the threat of black men having sexual relations with white women. During World War II the Red Cross turned away blood donated by blacks because of widespread fear that it would transmit racial characteristics to the offspring of whites who had transfusions with it. About one-third of the people questioned in a 1944 survey thought blood from whites differed from blood from blacks.[15] When the United States Supreme Court finally struck down an antimiscegenation statute in the 1967 case of *Loving v. Virginia,* public reaction was muted only because opposition to racial intermarriage remained so strong that the absence of a statute prohibiting it had little more than symbolic effect.

A Catholic Marriage

In 1946 Andrea Perez and Sylvester Davis went to the Los Angeles County Clerk, J. F. Moroney, and applied for a marriage license. Ms. Perez indicated in the application for the license that she was white, and Mr. Davis indicated he was black.[16] The clerk refused to issue the license, invoking Civil Code section 69, which stated, "no license may be issued authorizing the marriage of a white person with a Negro, mulatto, Mongolian or member of the Malay race."[17] Perez and Davis certainly knew their application for a marriage license would be refused. Davis, who was a college graduate,[18] and Perez had decided, before making the application, to file suit, asking the court to command the clerk to issue the marriage license.

The couple hired attorney Daniel Marshall to represent them. Marshall had been outspoken in opposition to racial discrimination before taking the case. He

---

[14]Till was brutally killed by the husband and half brother of a woman whom Till asked for a date. Despite the killers' confessions, a Mississippi jury acquitted them.

[15]Sickels, *Race, Marriage and the Law,* 54.

[16]Marriage license applicants generally identified their race themselves. County clerks sometimes refused to issue marriage licenses because they believed the applicants were prohibited from marrying because of their race. With the important exception of Traynor, most of those involved in the case did not question the means of determining the race of marriage license applicants.

The news articles on the case generally described Davis as Negro and Ms. Perez as white. *Time* described her as "olive skinned." *Time,* October 11, 1948. The *Van Nuys News* described her as a "white woman of Mexican decent." *Van Nuys News,* November 4, 1948. Ms. Perez could not have escaped the effect of the antimiscegenation statute by identifying herself as Hispanic. Even if she had self-identified as Latina, the statute did not recognize that identification. It treated Hispanics as white.

[17]Perez v. Sharp, 32 Cal.2d 711, 712 (1948).

[18]*Los Angeles Times,* October 2, 1948.

was active in the Los Angeles chapter of the American Civil Liberties Union. He had signed the ACLU *amicus curiae* briefs in two 1947 cases regarding discrimination against Japanese Americans.[19] In 1946 he wrote an article in the *Los Angeles Bar Bulletin* supporting Proposition 11, the Fair Employment Practices Act, which prohibited employment discrimination based on race, nationality, and religion, and his language in that article reflected clearly his convictions on racial discrimination:

> A free democratic state and society, its institutions, foundations and traditions are menaced—gravely menaced—when large numbers of its members are refused economic opportunity because of . . . discrimination, a malignancy which, expanded and extended, leads as an historical fact, to the moral, political and economic death of the social order and civilization which imposes it.[20]

Marshall's views brought with them professional risks. Anticommunists within the bar labeled Marshall and many other like-minded lawyers as communist sympathizers.

Fred Okrand, volunteer attorney for the Los Angeles ACLU during the late 1940s and 1950s, remembered Marshall as very idealistic and involved in left-wing causes.[21] Marshall's association with the left did not, however, bring with it support for the *Perez* case. Although American Civil Liberties Union director Ernest Besig praised the Court's decision in *Perez* after the fact,[22] civil liberties organizations avoided involvement in the case.[23] Community support for the litigation came from an unexpected source—Catholics and the Catholic Church.

Perez and Davis were Catholic, and they attended the same church. Marshall, also a Catholic, was the "militant president of the Los Angeles Catholic Interracial Counsel," which sponsored the litigation.[24] Archbishop J. Francis McIntyre and the Catholic press publicly supported Perez and Davis.[25] The editor of the *The Monitor: The Official Organ of the Archdiocese of San Francisco*, called the *Perez* decision a "progressive step" and noted that "[a]lthough the entire democratic world went to war to defeat and destroy forever just such a thing as espoused by Hitler, few bothered to recognize that here in California

---

[19]Oyama v. California, 29 Cal.2d 164 (1947); Takahashi v. Fish and Game Commission, 30 Cal.2d 719 (1947).

[20]Daniel Marshall, "An Act to Abolish Discrimination," *Los Angeles Bar Bulletin,* Vol. 22 (October 1946).

[21]Phone interview with Fred Okrand by Ben Field, November 6, 1997.

[22]*The Sacramento Bee,* October 2, 1948; *San Francisco Chronicle,* October 2, 1948.

[23]*The Nation,* October 16, 1948.

[24]*America,* "Triumph over Racism," January 22, 1949; *The Monitor: The Official Organ of the Archdiocese of San Francisco,*" October 22, 1948.

[25]*Los Angeles Times,* October 2, 1948.

there was embodied in our laws similar concepts of race superiority."[26] *America (A Catholic Review of the Week)* also published a laudatory article about *Perez* entitled "Triumph over Racism."[27] For Perez, Davis, Marshall, and other Catholics, the case pitted religious freedom against racism. Although the final result discounted the religious facet of the case, Marshall's religious freedom argument would play a crucial part in the internal decision-making process of the Court.

A Brief History of Antimiscegenation

Antimiscegenation statutes existed in California almost from the inception of the state. In 1850 three related statutes, including the state's first antimiscegenation statute, were enacted. The other two statutes prohibited blacks, mulattoes, and Indians from giving evidence for or against a white person or giving any evidence in a case in which a white person was a party.[28] Civil Code section 60 stated, "[a]ll marriages of white person with negroes, Mongolians, members of the Malay race or mulattoes are illegal and void."[29] In 1901, the legislature amended the law to include a prohibition of marriage between whites and "Mongolians," meaning Asians, particularly Japanese and Chinese. The 1933 case of *Roldan v. Los Angeles County* held that section 60 did not prohibit marriages between whites and Filipinos.[30] As a result, in the same year, the legislature again amended the law to prohibit those marriages.

California's antimiscegenation statute was in no way unusual. As Charles Stanley, attorney for the Los Angeles County Clerk, pointed out in his various papers on the subject and as the Justice John Schenk noted in his dissent, antimiscegenation statutes had a long history of acceptance in the United States.[31] Both Stanley and Justice Schenk traced the prohibition on mixed marriage to the colonial period. In his 1931 study on miscegenation, *Race Mixture: Studies in Intermarriage and Miscegenation,* Edward Byron Reuter identified a 1661 Maryland statute as the first law regulating interracial sexual relations in America.[32] When the United States gained its independence, almost all the states had antimiscegenation statutes. After independence six southern states included a

---

[26] *The Monitor,* October 22, 1948.

[27] *America,* "Triumph over Racism," January 22, 1949.

[28] Perez, 32 Cal.2d at 719.

[29] *Ibid.,* 712.

[30] Roldan v. Los Angeles County, 129 Cal.App. 267 (1933).

[31] Perez, 32 Cal.2d at 747–48; Perez Court File (California State Archives), Respondents Brief in Opposition to Writ of Mandate, October 6, 1947.

[32] Edward Byron Reuter, *Race Mixture: Studies in Intermarriage and Miscegenation* (New York, 1931), 78.

prohibition of miscegenation in their constitutions.[33] A few states repealed their antimiscegenation statutes, but most remained in place until the 1950s and 1960s.[34] From 1880 to 1920 legislatures in 12 plains and western states adopted antimiscegenation statutes.[35] The Progressive Era saw a surge of support for antimiscegenation statutes as seven states attempted to institute new prohibitions on interracial marriage.[36] In 1948, 30 states in addition to California had antimiscegenation statutes.

Antimiscegenation statutes were widely accepted in 1948. One of Stanley's briefs in *Perez* claimed that even in the 18 states that lacked antimiscegenation statutes "there have been frequent proposals that such laws be passed."[37] Stanley argued that the fact that nine of the 10 states to prohibit marriage between whites and "Mongolians" were west of the Mississippi was "another indication of the fact that this type of legislation is but the reflection of the community's attitude toward an alien minority group."[38] Polling data supported this claim. Not only whites, but minority communities as well, disdained interracial marriage. Black-white couples lived on the margins of the black community.[39] Members of the Nisei generation of Japanese Americans in California, and, to an even greater extent, members of the Sansei generation, had to overcome the resistance of their parents toward interracial marriage.[40]

Resistance to miscegenation varied depending on the races of the couple seeking a marriage license. Black-white couples had particular difficulty obtaining marriage licenses, even in states that lacked antimiscegenation statutes. When a white woman and a black man applied for a marriage license in Washington state, where there was no antimiscegenation statute, the county auditor, rejected their application. The auditor claimed he had the authority to determine the mental soundness of applicants and that any white woman who would marry a black man must be insane. She was, therefore, ineligible for a marriage license.[41] When it came to Asian Americans, on the other hand, the enforcement of California's antimiscegenation statute was lax after World War II, particularly in Los Angeles County. In Los Angeles County from 1924 to 1933, less than three percent of Japanese American men married non-Japanese women, and

---

[33]Those states were Alabama, Florida, Mississippi, North Carolina, South Carolina, and Tennessee. Reuter, *Race Mixture,* 82.

[34]The Maine, Massachusetts, Michigan, Ohio, and Pennsylvania state legislatures repealed their antimiscegenation statutes. Spikard, *Mixed Blood,* 286.

[35]Spikard, *Mixed Blood,* 286.

[36]*Ibid.,* 288.

[37]Perez Court File, Respondent's Brief in Opposition to Writ of Mandate.

[38]*Ibid.*

[39]Spikard, *Mixed Blood,* 302.

[40]*Ibid.*

[41]Perez Court File, Respondent's Brief in Opposition to Writ of Mandate, citing an anecdote from Reuter, *Race Mixture.*

1.7 percent of Japanese American women married non-Japanese men.[42] The Sansei generation married whites with far greater frequency. After World War II one-fourth of the interracial marriages in Los Angeles County were illegal unions between Japanese Americans and whites.[43] Marriages between whites and Mexicans also could be interracial, but they were legal. As numerous commentators have observed, the main objective of antimiscegenation statutes was to prevent the union of black men and white women. "A white woman's relation with a Negro man," Gunnar Myrdal wrote, "is met by the full fury of antiamalgamation sanctions."[44]

Legal Precedent for Antimiscegenation Statutes

In 1948 state and federal courts had already heard challenges to antimiscegenation statutes, and they upheld those statutes without exception. The dissenters in *Perez,* citing federal and state cases, noted that the "authorities form an unbroken line of judicial support, both state and federal, for the validity of our own legislation, and there is none to the contrary."[45] The 1944 federal case of *Stevens v. United States* upheld an Oklahoma antimiscegenation statute on the grounds that marriage was not a right protected by the 14th Amendment.[46] The United States Supreme Court addressed a related set of issues in the case of *Pace v. Alabama,* which involved a challenge to an Alabama statute that punished interracial adultery more severely than adultery between members of the same race.[47] The Court held that the statute did not violate the 14th Amendment Equal Protection Clause because it applied to blacks and whites equally. Numerous state courts upheld antimiscegenation statutes on similar grounds or on the grounds that marriage was not a right protected by the 14th Amendment, and attorney Charles Stanley made both arguments in *Perez.*

California precedents provided no support for Ms. Perez's position either. The first antimiscegenation case to arise in California involved a manumitted slave who had married her former master in 1854 in the Territory of Utah.[48] Utah did not prohibit racial intermarriage at the time. The California Supreme Court uncritically accepted the California antimiscegenation statute, but held the marriage valid because it was lawful in Utah. In 1933 the Court of Appeals applied the antimiscegenation statute, but held that the statute did not cover "Ma-

---

[42]Spikard, *Mixed Blood,* 48.

[43]*Ibid.,* 70.

[44]Myrdal, *An American Dilemma,* 56.

[45]Perez, 32 Cal.2d at 752.

[46]Stevens v. United States, 146 Fed.2d 120, 123 (1944).

[47]Pace v. Alabama, 106 U.S. 583 (1883).

[48]Pearson v. Pearson, 51 Cal.120 (1875).

lays."[49] The legislature responded to the court's invitation by amending the statute to include them.

Two 1941 California Court of Appeals cases raised the issue of the validity of racial intermarriage. *Estate of Stark* involved a contest over the will of Abagail Stark.[50] Abagail was the daughter of Robert Stark and his mulatto slave Catherine, who had lived with Robert in California as his common-law wife. Robert had children by a prior marriage, and, when Abagail died, they contested her will. The Court of Appeals in Los Angeles held that Abagail was illegitimate because the antimiscegenation statute prohibited her parents' marriage. As a result, the court held that the law of wills did not recognize a relationship between Abagail and the legitimate offspring of her father; the offspring of Robert Stark's prior marriage were not Abagail's heirs and, therefore, could not contest her will.

Although *Stark* did not present a direct challenge to the constitutionality of the antimiscegenation statute, it did present opportunities for the Court of Appeals to find it inapplicable. The statute failed to define mulatto so the Court of Appeals had to import a definition from elsewhere. The statute did not specifically apply to "marriages of consent"; the Court of Appeals had to find that the statute applied even though Catherine and Robert Stark never formalized their marriage and had lived together well before they entered California. Instead of questioning the validity of the antimiscegenation statute, the Court of Appeals went out of its way to apply it.

In *Estate of Monks,* tne second 1941 miscegenation case, the Court of Appeals in San Diego specifically addressed a challenge to the constitutionality of an antimiscegenation statute.[51] The case revolved around a marriage between Antoinette Giraudo and Allan Monks. When Monks died, he willed everything to Ms. Giraudo, but a probate court ruled that she obtained the will by fraud and that her marriage to Monks was void. The two had married in Arizona, which prohibited anyone of white ancestry from marrying a nonwhite. The probate court determined that Mr. Monks was white and that Ms. Giraudo had one-eighth Negro blood and therefore was a mulatto though she claimed to be a French countess. Ms. Giraudo's attorney argued that the antimiscegenation statute was "repugnant to the Fourteenth Amendment to the Constitution of the United States in that it deprives her and others of her racial classification of liberty to contract marriage."[52] The Court evaded this challenge, ruling that, because Ms. Giraudo was free to marry a nonwhite, no constitutional issue was

[49]Roldan, 129 Cal.App. 267.

[50]Estate of Stark, 48 Cal.2d 209 (1941).

[51]Estate of Monks, 48 Cal.App.2d 603, 612 (1941).

[52]*Ibid.,* 612. The phrase "liberty to contract" has often been associated with late nineteenth- and early twentieth-century liberalism. Neither the parties in *Perez v. Sharp* nor the justices used this phrase.

"squarely presented."[53] When *Perez v. Sharp* came before the California Supreme Court, the Court itself had recently heard other cases involving race-
based legal classifications. In the 1946 case of *People v. Oyama,* the Court
unanimously upheld California's Alien Land Law that prohibited Japanese
Americans who were ineligible for citizenship from owning land.[54] Traynor indicated his dissatisfaction with the result in a one sentence concurrence, stating
simply that he felt bound by a previous U.S. Supreme Court decision upholding
the statute. In 1947, *Takahashi v. Fish and Game Commission* brought before
the Court a constitutional challenge to the California Fish and Game Code that
barred Japanese Americans ineligible for citizenship from obtaining commercial
fishing licenses.[55] A majority of the Court upheld the statute, but both Traynor
and Chief Justice Gibson joined Justice Carter's strong dissent.

Two years earlier in the 1944 case of *Fairchild v. Raines,* Traynor concurred with Justice Rey Schauer's majority opinion refusing to enforce a restrictive covenant.[56] Ross and Helen Raines, a black couple, had been prevented by a
lower court from using land in Pasadena because of a covenant restricting the
use of the land to whites. Housing for blacks surrounded the land covered by
restrictive covenants. Neither Schauer nor Traynor found the covenant legally
invalid per se. In keeping with previously decided cases, they held that race-
based restrictions against the occupancy of land by people of color could be enforced in certain cases. However, the covenant could not be enforced unless the
lower court considered the changed character of the neighborhood and the public interests involved.

Traynor's opinion in *Fairchild* showed an expansive view of the public interest. Citing sociological and historical literature on the problem of racial segregation in urban areas, he expressed sympathy for blacks who migrated from
the South "in response to the increasing demands of industry for labor."[57] "Negroes migrating into urban communities have found barriers at every turn," he
wrote, "Race restrictions . . . must yield to the public interest in the sound development of the whole community."[58] Traynor opposed restrictive covenants. Although he felt compelled to abide by the precedent that allowed them, he also
expressed the view that the courts had a responsibility to solve "the problem of
race segregation."[59] His opinion in *Fairchild* demonstrated his willingness to use
the power of the Court to pursue racial integration.

---

[53]*Ibid.*
[54]People v. Oyama, 29 Cal.2d 164 (1946).
[55]Takahashi v. Fish and Game Commission, 30 Cal.2d 719 (1947).
[56]Fairchild v. Raines, 24 Cal.2d 818 (1944).
[57]*Ibid.,* 834.
[58]*Ibid.*
[59]*Ibid.,* 833.

Traynor supported an active role for the Court in promoting integration throughout his tenure on the bench. In the 1967 case of *Reitman v. Mulkey*, the Court, with Traynor as chief justice, struck down as unconstitutional an initiative (Proposition 14) that prohibited the state from interfering with the right of landlords and home sellers to discriminate on the basis of race.[60] The Court ruled that Proposition 14 violated the Fourteenth Amendment by putting the state in the position of encouraging racial discrimination. Traynor signed on to the majority opinion, written by Justice Peek. The U.S. Supreme Court reviewed the case and upheld the California Court's decision. However, a backlash against the California Supreme Court followed its decision to strike down the popular initiative. The decision prompted a campaign to oust the justices. Although the campaign failed, Traynor felt the political pressure resulting from the court's unpopular move.[61] He realized the Court would come under attack, but felt strongly enough about Proposition 14 to strike it down despite the political consequences.

The Climate of Opinion Surrounding the *Perez* Case

Traynor's decision to invalidate California's miscegenation statute lacked legal precedent. Although a growing body of scientific literature supported his decision, the legislature only needed a "rational basis" for the antimiscegenation statute. Stanley, the Los Angeles County Clerk's attorney, argued that contemporary scientific data on racial attributes and the effects of interracial breeding provided the necessary "rational basis." "There is certainly adequate biological data," he wrote, "which has been sufficient to convince certain of the authorities both that the crossing of widely different races has undesirable [*sic*] biological results and that the Negro race is biologically inferior to the white in certain important respects."[62] Stanley's brief cited scientific evidence that blacks were more prone to disease than whites, particularly dental ulcers and gangrenous decay, that blacks suffered from sickle cell anemia, that blacks were more prone to alcoholism and insanity than whites, and that blacks had a higher mortality rate than whites.[63] Stanley also cited scientific evidence that the offspring of blacks and whites were weaker than their parents and infertile.[64] A central theme of popular racial mythology was that interracial mixture caused the degeneracy of both races. J. W. Gregory's *The Menace of Colour* expressed this common misconception and provided a source of data on the inferiority of mulattos cited

---

[60]Reitman v. Mulkey, 387 U.S 369 (1967), 64 Cal.2d 529 (1967).
[61]Interview with Adrian Kragen by Ben Field, August 15, 1997.
[62]Perez Court File, Brief in Opposition to Writ of Mandate.
[63]*Ibid.;* Perez, 32 Cal.2d at 757.
[64]Perez Court File, Brief in Opposition to Writ of Mandate.

by both Stanley and the dissent in *Perez*.[65] Finally, Stanley cited various cases from southern states for the proposition that the inferiority of blacks was judicially recognized.[66]

Ms. Perez's attorney, Daniel Marshall, contended that there was no support in genetics for Stanley's arguments about the biological inferiority of blacks and mulattos.[67] However, he spent few words rebutting Stanley's "biological considerations." Justice Traynor's curtness with Stanley during oral argument suggested that Traynor did not need to be persuaded that these "biological considerations" lacked merit. When Stanley said during oral argument, "The white race is superior physically and mentally to the black race and the intermarriage of these races results in a lessening of physical and mental vitality in their offspring," Traynor responded incredulously "Are there medical men in this country today who say such a thing?"[68] As Traynor explained in his opinion, he did not believe proof of the biological inferiority of blacks existed.

Traynor could not, however, point to consensus within the scientific community on the equality of blacks and whites. Daniel Marshall did not even argue the point. Edward Reuter had written in 1931 "It appears to be fairly well established as a biological fact that, as such, neither inbreeding nor outbreeding has any beneficial or injurious consequences."[69] However, Reuter also acknowledged that "many writers, striving for popularity, have exploited the doctrine (of white supremacy) to an uninformed and eager audience. There has grown up a considerable body of pseudoscientific literature that stimulates at the same time that it caters to popular beliefs and prejudices."[70] Mainstream texts on genetics, such as Dr. C. Stern's 1949 *Principles of Human Genetics,* found no support for theories of white superiority.[71] However, the debate over the causes of the disparity in the standardized test scores of black children and white children sustained the belief in the genetic inferiority of blacks. School desegregation in the 1950s and 1960s fueled the controversy. In the 1967 case of *Loving v. Virginia,* Virginia Attorney General Gernal Button, defending Virginia's antimiscegenation statute, cited to the U.S. Supreme Court many of the scientific materials cited by the dissent in *Perez*. As late as 1969 the *Harvard Educational Review*

---

[65] *Ibid.*

[66] *Ibid.*

[67] Perez Court File, Petitioner's Reply Brief.

[68] Perez Court File, Transcript of Oral Argument, 3.

[69] Reuter, *Race Mixture,* 5.

[70] *Ibid.,* 12.

[71] Sickels, *Race, Marriage and the Law,* 56.

would publish an article that imputed the difference between the IQ scores of blacks and whites largely to genetic differences.[72]

Stanley argued not only that scientific research supported the antimiscegenation statute, but that social conditions required it. He wrote in argument, "The courts cannot shut their eyes to conditions which are everywhere about them as part of the social order and domestic economy of the State. They may properly take judicial notice of the relation existing between the white and the colored races of the state."[73] The strident tone of his argument suggested that Stanley believed his "sociological considerations" were so convincing or so widely accepted that the Court would not dare to contravene them. Stanley could have emphasized the more cautious argument—ultimately articulated by dissenting Justice Schenk—that the legislature needed only a "rational basis" to pass a constitutional antimiscegenation statute. Stanley did make this argument too, but it is far less prominent than the lengthy "sociological considerations" section of his brief, which treats the antimiscegenation statute as good policy supported by obvious, uncontroverted social concerns.

Stanley contended that racial intermarriage not only raised societal race tensions, but damaged the institution of marriage. Citing a pseudoscientific 1937 study by Dr. Samuel J. Holmes, a University of California professor of zoology, called "Negro's Struggle for Survival,"[74] Stanley argued that miscegenation caused a host of marriage and family problems. "The principal reason, and one which I think fully justifies the Legislature in having acted against this type of marriage," Stanley said in oral argument, "is the sociological one that it places such a strain on the marital relation and family ties and puts the offspring in such an unfavorable position that, until the people of the State have changed their opinions and their mores to such an extent that they instruct their Legislature to repeal this law, we need such a law."[75]

Stanley played on fears that tensions between blacks and whites in California were becoming increasingly acute. During World War II tens of thousands of blacks had migrated to California to work in war industries. Stanley pointed to the influx of blacks as a source of tension that could erupt into violence. "Before the war there were 60,000 Negroes jammed into the colored quarter around Central Avenue [Los Angeles]," he wrote, "The population has now grown to 180,000 and the Negroes have almost no opportunity to spread. . . . Fear of ra-

---

[72]See Sickels, *Race, Marriage and the Law,* 61, describing Arthur Jensen, "How Much Can We Boost IQ and Scholastic Achievement?" *Harvard Educational Review* (Winter 1969).

[73]Perez Court File, Return by Way of Demurrer and Points and Authorities, October 6, 1947.

[74]Perez Court File, Brief in Opposition to Writ of Mandate, citing Samuel J. Holmes, *The Negro's Struggle for Survival, A Study in Human Ecology* (Berkeley, 1937).

[75]Perez Court File, Transcript of Oral Argument, October 6, 1947, 8.

cial troubles is so great that for several years the Los Angeles police and sher-
iff's office have had complete plans worked out for quelling a riot before it
could get started."[76] Stanley's vision of race relations involved clear lines of
separation between blacks and whites with the forces of the state clearly under
white control.

Stanley took the position that blacks and Catholics, like other more powerful racial and religious groups, had an interest in maintaining lines of racial
separation. In his vision of race relations, minorities acquiesced in their separation from whites. Stanley pointed out that racial intermarriage troubled blacks as
well as whites. He even quoted "eminent Negro educator" W.E.B. DuBois from
his article "Social Equality and Racial Intermarriage" for the proposition that
miscegenation was inadvisable because of racial animosity and the need to preserve black culture.[77] Perez and Davis were Catholic, and their attorney had insisted that their marriage was a matter of religious freedom and obligation.
Stanley responded by citing Father John LaFarge, former associate editor of the
right-wing national Catholic weekly *American*. With the approval of the Catholic Church, LaFarge had written two books on race relations and Catholic doctrine, arguing against interracial marriage on the grounds that the social stigma
associated with it created an obstacle to healthy family life.[78] Stanley used the
Catholic Church's opposition to miscegenation to blunt Ms. Perez's call for religious freedom.[79]

Ms. Perez's attorney, Marshall, did little to refute Stanley's "sociological
considerations." Oral argument made it clear that at least two justices—Traynor
and Carter—had different sociological considerations in mind. During oral argument Traynor raised an issue that Marshall had not raised, one that originated
in Traynor's social science readings. Noting that racial labels like Negro and
mulatto were not defined by California statute, Traynor asked whether these
labels were unconstitutionally vague and uncertain. As the following colloquy
between Traynor and Stanley demonstrated, Traynor recognized the anthropological difficulties with the concept of race:

Traynor: . . . it might help to explain the statute, what it means. What is a negro?

---

[76]Perez Court File, Brief in Opposition to Writ of Mandate.
[77]*Ibid.*
[78]John LaFarge, *Interracial Justice (A Study of Catholic Doctrine of Race Relations),* (New York, 1937); John LaFarge, *The Race Question and the Negro (A Study of
Catholic Doctrine of Interracial Justice),* (New York, 1943).
[79]Perez Court File, Return by Way of Answer, October 6, 1947.

Stanley: We have not the benefit of any judicial interpretation. The statute states that a negro [*sic*] cannot marry a negro, which can be construed to mean a full-blooded negro, since the statute also says mulatto, Mongolian or Malay.

Traynor: What is a mulatto? One-sixteenth blood?

Stanley: Certainly certain states have seen fit to state what a mulatto is.

Traynor: If there is 1/8 blood, can they marry? If you can marry with 1/8, why not with 1/16, 1/32, 1/64? And then don't you get in the ridiculous position where a negro cannot marry anybody? If he is white, he cannot marry black, or if he is black, he cannot marry white.

Stanley: I agree that it would be better for the Legislature to lay down the exact amount of blood, but I do not think that the statute should be declared unconstitutional as indefinite on this ground.

Traynor: That is something anthropologists have not been able to furnish, although they say generally that there is no such thing as race.

Stanley: I would not say that anthropologists have said that generally, except such statements for sensational purposes.

Traynor: Would you say that Professor Wooten [*sic*] of Harvard was a sensationalist? The crucial question is how can a county clerk determine who are negroes and who are whites?[80]

Traynor recognized that Stanley's expression "full-blooded negro" carried a great deal of conceptual baggage. It appears Traynor intended to refer to Harvard anthropologist Earnest Hooten toward the end of his exchange with Stanley. Professor Hooten, like many contemporary social scientists, explored the difficulties in defining race. As Gunnar Myrdal pointed out in *An American Dilemma,* "the concept of the American Negro is a social concept and not a biological one."[81] "In modern biological and ethnological research 'race' as a scientific concept has lost sharpness of meaning," Myrdal wrote, "and the term is disappearing in sober writings."[82]

Hooten's ideas about race placed him in line with a group of contemporary social scientists broadly described as assimilationist. Led by University of Chicago sociologist Robert Park, the assimilationists envisioned the end of race relations in the United States. Reuter was a student of Park, as were several

---

[80]Perez Court File, Transcript of Oral Argument, 3–4.

[81]Myrdal, *An American Dilemma,* 136.

[82]*Ibid.,* 115.

other influential social scientists of Traynor's day. When Traynor decided *Perez*, assimilationist ideas had gained widespread acceptance among anthropologists. As Ralph Linton, president of the American Anthropological Association, noted in an address to his colleagues, "most anthropologists agree there will be no Negro problem in another two hundred years; by then there will not be enough recognizable Negroes in the country to constitute a problem."[83] The assimilationists believed that blacks had lost their African cultural heritage, largely because of slavery, and that blacks were in the process of losing their physical distinctiveness. They theorized that black men sought to marry lighter skinned black women, and that this demand would result in increasingly light skinned offspring each generation. Assimilationists pointed to census findings that suggested the black population was growing lighter.[84] A corollary assimilationist theory, which comforted whites, was Professor Hooten's assertion that a white person and a person who passed for white could not produce black offspring.[85] Thus, as the black population became whiter and gradually passed, they would not "pollute" the white population.[86] The writings of the assimilationists made racial egalitarianism more palatable to white liberals, and Justice Traynor would cite their theories directly in his *Perez* opinion.

The *Perez* Case and Judicial Commitment to Racial Equality

Traynor's opinion in *Perez* undeniably broke with precedent, and Traynor made no effort to disguise the novelty of his decision. Unlike Perez's attorney, Traynor never contended that the constitutionality of the statute was "an issue of first impression."[87] He used the standard "rational basis" test to determine whether the antimiscegenation statute violated the Equal Protection Clause of the Constitution: the issue was whether the race-based restrictions were a "reasonable means" to achieve a "legitimate legislative objective."[88] Traynor found that California courts had given a consistent affirmative answer to this question from the 1854 case of *People v. Hall* to the most contemporary judicial prece-

---

[83]As quoted in Williamson, *The New People*, 123.

[84]Spikard, *Mixed Blood*, 271.

[85]Earnest Hooten, "The Antropometry of Some Small Samples of Negroes and Negroids," in Caroline Bond Day, ed., *A Study of Some Negro White Families in the United States* (Cambridge Massachusetts, 1932), 107.

[86]Williamson, *The New People*, 127.

[87]Perez Court File, Petition for a Writ of Mandamus, Memorandum of Points and Authorities, August 8, 1947.

[88]Perez, 32 Cal.2d at 713, 718.

dent supporting the statute, the 1941 case of *Estate of Stark*.[89] However, his analysis located the historical origins of the antimiscegenation statute in a form of race prejudice undisguised by justifications dealing with public health or social peace, and he could not abide by this bald judicial assertion of racist sentiment.

Traynor did not discuss the precedents supporting antimiscegenation statutes in other states since those cases did not control his decision. Neither did he discuss the 1944 federal case of *Stevens v. United States,* which upheld an Oklahoma antimiscegenation statute.[90] He felt compelled to deal with *Pace v. Alabama,* the 1883 U.S. Supreme Court case that came closest to the issue in *Perez,* but only to find the case inapplicable.[91] *Pace* upheld a conviction under an Alabama statute that outlawed all extramarital sexual relations, but imposed a greater penalty for interracial sex. Traynor distinguished the case on the grounds that it dealt with adultery rather than marriage.[92]

One measure of the extent to which Traynor's opinion broke with precedent is the contrast between it, the dissent, and the arguments of counsel in the case. Justice Shenk's dissent was more conventional than Traynor's opinion in both method and substance. Shenk set forth the issue in the case, summarized the parties' positions, cited the case law on miscegenation—which uniformly supported the California statute—and drew his conclusion. Although Shenk's dissenting opinion generally mirrored Stanley's arguments, Shenk placed more emphasis on precedent and less emphasis on the scientific and sociological support for the statute.

Shenk held an antiactivist's view of the role of the courts and the legislature. "Courts are neither peculiarly qualified nor organized to determine the underlying questions of fact with reference to which the validity of the legislation must be determined," he wrote.[93] Judges lacked the expertise and the institutional policymaking capacity to make good policy. Moreover, Shenk stated, judicial policymaking was undemocratic. "What the people's legislative representatives believe to be for the public good must be accepted as tending to promote the public welfare," he wrote. "It has been said that any other basis would conflict with the spirit of the Constitution and would sanction measures opposed to a republican form of government."[94] Shenk asserted that a scientific and sociological basis for the statute existed, but, unlike Stanley, he did not bank on its correctness. Instead, he insisted that scientific and sociological evidence was

---

[89]People v. Hall, 4 Cal. 399, 404 (1854); Estate of Stark, 48 Cal.App.2d 209, 214 (1941).

[90]Stevens v. United States, 146 Fed.2d 120, 123 (1944).

[91]Pace v. Alabama, 106 U.S. 583 (1883).

[92]Perez, 32 Cal.2d at 726.

[93]*Ibid.,* 755.

[94]Perez, 32 Cal.2d at 756.

sufficient to justify the Court's deference to the legislative decision enacting the antimiscegenation law.

Stanley made white superiority the heart of his argument. "The . . . evidence that the Legislature had," he said in oral argument, "is that there is a definite showing—I do not like to say it or to tie myself in with 'Mein Kampf'—but it has been shown that the white race is superior physically and mentally to the black race, and the intermarriage of these races results in a lessening of physical vitality and mentality in their offspring."[95] Instead of taking a conventional approach by relying on the unbroken line of precedent supporting his position, Stanley—with some embarrassment—insisted on the correctness of the policy underlying the antimiscegenation statute.

Stanley's white supremacy argument generated visceral reactions from Marshall. In his written arguments to the court he compared Stanley's position with the racial doctrines articulated in *Mein Kampf* and invoked the memory of American soldiers who fought against Hitler in World War II.[96] For strategic reasons of his own, Marshall attempted to define the issues in nonracial terms. He repeatedly emphasized that the antimiscegenation statute infringed on the religious freedom of his clients. His main argument was that the statute denied Perez and Davis a sacrament and therefore impinged on their free exercise of religion.[97] As Stanley pointed out in the opening lines of his oral argument, if the antimiscegenation statute restricted the free exercise of religion it had to pass the "clear and present danger" test. Without "clear and present danger" of an evil that the legislature had the right to prevent, the statute would be unconstitutional. The "clear and present danger" test required far less deference to the legislature than the "rational basis" test. As Stanley noted, one reason Marshall made the religious freedom argument was to gain the strategic advantage of the stricter test.

The religious affiliations of the justices provided a second strategic reason for Marshall's religious freedom argument. Marshall may have considered Traynor sympathetic to his clients because, like them, Traynor was Catholic. Marshall may also have tailored his religious freedom argument to appeal to Justice Douglas Edmonds. Justice Edmonds generally voted with the socially conservative justices on the Court, Shenk, Shauer, and Spence; and so Court watchers expected him to vote with them in *Perez*. Edmonds was, however, a devoted Christian Scientist who felt strongly about religious liberty.[98] Although Traynor rejected Marshall's religious freedom argument, it appealed to Ed-

---

[95]Perez Court File, Transcript of Oral Argument, 6.

[96]Perez Court File, Answer to the Petition for Rehearing, October 21, 1948.

[97]Perez Court File, Petition for a Writ of Mandamus, Memorandum of Point and Authorities, August 8, 1947.

[98]Interview with Don Barrett by Ben Field, May 24, 1997.

monds, the swing vote in the case, and Edmonds based his concurring opinion on it.

The most obvious difference between Marshall's "rational basis" argument and Traynor's opinion was that Marshall paid little attention to the scientific and sociological debate surrounding race mixing. He cited very little evidence to refute Stanley's "biological considerations" and "sociological considerations." Traynor read and cited various scientific and sociological texts independently of any suggestion by the lawyers. Unlike Marshall, Traynor built his analysis on an awareness of contemporary anthropological thinking.[99] He used the phrase "so-called races" in his opinion,[100] and he observed, that anthropologists "say generally that there is no such thing as race."[101] Marshall used the phrase "the so-called white race" in oral argument, suggesting some awareness of the difficulties involved in clearly defining race. However, Traynor, and not Marshall, attached legal significance to the nebulousness of the concept of race. He asserted that the racial classifications in the statute were unconstitutionally vague and uncertain.

The bulk of Traynor's opinion was not a discussion of precedent, but a "reasonable means" analysis of the statute. His law clerk, Don Barrett, advised him that the requirements of this analysis were so minimal that invalidating the statute would be difficult. Barrett thought Traynor should attack the statute as a violation of broad constitutional principles, as Justice Carter did in his concurring opinion.[102] Quoting from the Declaration of Independence, the Fifth and Fourteenth Amendments to the Constitution, and the Charter of the United Nations, Carter urged that race equality was a matter of "fundamental law."[103] "The wisdom of the broad, liberal concept of liberty and equality declared in our fundamental law should be apparent to every unprejudiced mind," he wrote.[104] Carter flamboyantly quoted the Apostle Paul, Thomas Jefferson, Hitler, and Lord Nottingham. He referred to the Civil War and World War II as part of an American heritage of sacrifice for the principle of racial equality.

Traynor abstained from such sweeping historical interpretations, and he carefully avoided grounding his arguments in anything so amorphous as "fundamental law." He expressed himself in concrete terms; phrases like the "broad, liberal concept of liberty and equality" do not appear in his opinion. Instead, he pointed out the logical flaws in the statute. He showed that if the statute intended to establish a proscription against mixed blood marriages, it did so poorly. It prohibited marriages between whites and "Negroes, Mongolians, mulattos, or

---

[99]Perez Case File, Oral Argument in Support of the Petition, October 6, 1947, 2.

[100]Perez, 32 Cal.2d at 721.

[101]Perez Case File, Transcript of Oral Argument, 4.

[102]Interview of Don Barrett by Ben Field, May 24, 1997.

[103]Perez, 32 Cal.2d at 733.

[104]*Ibid.*

Malays" but not "others of darker pigmentation, such as Indians, Hindus, or Mexicans."[105] Traynor questioned Stanley on this point during oral argument. "What you have to establish," he told Stanley, "is not the validity of a law preventing mixed marriages or races generally, but a law prohibiting the mixing of Caucasians with any of the specified colored races."[106] The law did not even prohibit marriages between "white and colored blood" because people whose ancestry was partly or even mostly white could, if they were not classified as white, marry nonwhites.[107] Traynor played down his objection to the racism of the statute, emphasizing instead that it was not a "reasonable means" of achieving a "legislative objective."

Traynor looked beneath the race labels the statute used. He observed that a "predominance in number of ancestors of one race" did not actually determine a person's race because that person might exhibit physical characteristics commonly associated with a different race. Traynor recognized that conceptions of race stemmed from societal practices, not family lineage. Although the California antimiscegenation statute did not define the terms white, Negro, Mongolian, mulatto, or Malay, historically antimiscegenation statutes defined race by ancestry. Stanley argued that a mulatto was a person with one-eighth part or more Negro blood.[108] Traynor suggested that a person with less than one-eighth part black blood might still exhibit physical characteristics of a black ancestor, "effectively precluding his marriage to another white person."[109] Traynor acknowledged that societal conceptions of race constrained choices of marital partners. However, the proscriptions of the antimiscegenation statute required clear definitions of race, which did not exist.

Although Traynor avoided explicit statements of broad principle, his analysis revealed his inclinations on race issues. After pointing out the logical flaws in the antimiscegenation statute, he weighed the scientific and sociological evidence for and against the statute, devoting more space to this discussion than any other issue in the case. Citing Professor Ralph Linton and other assimilationist social scientists, he concluded that "modern experts are agreed that the progeny of marriages between persons of different races are not inferior to both parents."[110] Traynor, like the assimilationists, foresaw racial harmony in the future. "There are now so many persons in the United States of mixed ancestry," Traynor wrote, "that the tensions upon them are already diminishing and are

[105]Perez, 32 Cal.2d at 721.
[106]Perez Case File, Transcript of Oral Argument, 5.
[107]*Ibid.*
[108]Perez Case File, Supplemental Points and Authorities in Support of Demurrer, November 19, 1947.
[109]Perez, 32 Cal.2d at 731.
[110]*Ibid.,* 720.

bound to diminish even more with time."[111] The footnote to this expression of assimilationist optimism revealed the influence of Reuter's *Race Mixture* and Professor Melville Herskovits's *The Antropometry of the American Negro*. Herskovits's book was one of the most influential statements of the assimilationist school of thought. He studied the genealogical composition of American blacks and concluded that over 70 percent had white ancestors. Traynor's references to Linton, Reuter, and Herskovits indicated his openness to their assimilationist tenets.

The text most frequently cited in Traynor's opinion was Gunnar Myrdal's *An American Dilemma: The Negro Problem and Modern Democracy;* Traynor cited it five times in his opinion. Myrdal was a Swedish social economist who received a Carnegie Corporation grant to study "the Negro question" in the United States. His unsettling insights into American race relations quickly gained widespread attention. He contrasted the social reality of racial prejudice against blacks with the "American Creed"—"a humanistic liberalism," "centered in the belief in equality and the rights to liberty."[112] Although Myrdal's observations on the realities of race in the United States often seemed harsh, he had great faith in the "American Creed." "What America is constantly reaching for is democracy at home and abroad," he wrote. "The main trend in its history is the gradual realization of the American Creed."[113] Myrdal believed that the post-World War II era provided a unique opportunity to overcome racial prejudice. Blacks had become "educated and culturally assimilated."[114] World War II destroyed the respectability of white supremacy for upper-class and well-educated white people; Myrdal saw "the gradual destruction of the popular theory behind race prejudice."[115] He rejected assimilationist conclusions about the genetic amalgamation of blacks. He criticized Melville Herskovits's research on African-American genealogy and concluded "there are no reasons to believe that a more complete amalgamation between whites and Negroes will occur within the surveyable future."[116] However, Myrdal's observations jibed with assimilationist conclusions in a broader sense. Myrdal, like the assimilationists, believed blacks were becoming integrated into American society.

Although by 1948 most social scientists had rejected theories of white supremacy,[117] longstanding and deeply entrenched ideas about race still supported the antimiscegenation statute. Traynor could have deferred to this tradition of racial separation, but chose not to. He believed the antimiscegenation statute

---

[111] *Ibid.,* 727.

[112] Myrdal, *An American Dilemma,* 8.

[113] *Ibid.,* 1021.

[114] *Ibid.,* 1022.

[115] *Ibid.,* 1002–03.

[116] *Ibid.,* 136.

[117] Williamson, *The New People,* 135.

lacked a "legitimate legislative objective" because its assumptions about race had been refuted by contemporary science and social science. According to his associates and clerks, Traynor abhorred racism, though he did not explicitly condemn the antimiscegenation statute on principle. His decision to avoid sweeping pronouncements of racial equality revealed a strategy of judicial prudence. He used a rationalistic approach in *Perez* to create an impression of scientific neutrality.

The Reaction to the *Perez* Case

Perez received significant attention in California newspapers. Most, if not all, daily newspapers in the state covered the case; many published front-page articles about it. Several articles noted that California was alone in ruling that the ban on mixed marriages was unconstitutional or commented that the Court had rejected longstanding precedent.[118] Some articles, such as one appearing in the *Los Angeles Daily Journal* entitled "Negro-White Marriage Sanctioned" suggested that the Court favored interracial marriages.[119] However, most of the state's newspapers published articles that dispassionately described the decision.[120] A *San Jose Mercury News* article was probably representative of newsroom thinking when it commented that interracial marriage would not cause genetic problems, but that it created social difficulties.[121] The article went on to ask whether the Court's decision would cause "dire social consequences," and it answered,

> It is doubtful if any American law rests upon more deeply rooted mores than do the statutes against interracial marriages. Such marriages are rare in the 19 states that do not bar them legally. . . . Standing as it does within the framework of contemporary social forces the California decision looks more like a somewhat abstract victory for individual freedom—a freedom likely to be claimed

[118]See e.g., *San Francisco Chronicle*, "Interracial Marriage: State Supreme Court Says Ban Unconstitutional," October 2, 1948; *San Francisco Examiner*, "Color Ban in Marriage Ruled Illegal," October 2, 1948; *Watsonville Register-Pajaronian*, October 4, 1948.

[119]*Los Angeles Daily Journal*, "Negro-White Marriage Sanctioned," October 4, 1948.

[120]See e.g., Associated Press Report in *San Jose News*, October 1, 1948; *San Bernardino Sun*, October 2, 1948; *Los Angeles Herald Express*, October 8, 1948; *Los Angeles Examiner*, October 3, 1948; *San Jose Mercury News*, October 2, 1948; *Los Angeles Herald and Express*, November 2, 1948; *San Francisco Call-Bulletin*, October 1, 1948; *San Francisco News*, October 1, 1948; and *Oakland Tribune*, October 1, 1948.

[121]*San Jose Mercury News*, "The Court Rules: Interracial Marriages," November 1, 1948.

by an exceptional few—than as a prelude to any substantial change in the American scene within the foreseeable future.[122]

Despite the controversial nature of interracial marriage, *Perez* generated little public reaction. The case did inspire some hate mail addressed to Traynor.[123] In one instance of open criticism, the former head of the State Bar, Frank Belcher, attacked the Court for wandering from the traditional judicial domain into politics, which he considered the legislature's purview.[124] Initially, too, several county clerks continued to ask applicants for marriage licenses to indicate their race, but this practice disappeared in the years following *Perez*.[125]

The experiences of American soldiers abroad during World War II affected their reaction to *Perez*. One newspaper column printed a mock conversation among former soldiers about the case.[126] When told about *Perez* one former soldier responded, "Boy that's good. A bunch o' guys I know 're gonna be awful sore they let some commandin' officers talk 'em out o' marryin' some of those Burmese gals." Another chimed in, "They sure were something." This anecdotal evidence of changing attitudes about some interracial marriages was supported by the increase in the number of interracial marriages after World War II.[127] The increase was, however, actually very small. Out of a total of 78,266 marriage licenses issued during the 30 months following *Perez,* the Los Angeles County Clerk issued only 455 licenses for marriages between a white person and a person of some other race.[128]

Scholarly commentary on *Perez* was surprisingly subdued. Most national law reviews mentioned *Perez* for the first time in the 1960s, if they mentioned the case at all. A note in 1963 in the *University of Virginia Law Review* assessed as negligible the impact of *Perez* on the South. Since *Perez,* the author observed, Virginia and Alabama had upheld antimiscegenation statutes and Louisiana and Mississippi had avoided ruling on the constitutionality of their antimiscegenation statutes in cases that raised the issue.[129] The author concluded without passion, "It seems doubtful that such statutes will survive the next U.S. Supreme Court test."[130] Law reviews in California gave *Perez* more attention. A student note in the *California Law Review* described the case as "ably written," a "revo-

---

[122]*Ibid.*

[123]Interview with Don Barrett by Ben Field, May 24, 1997.

[124]*Los Angeles Herald Express,* "High Court Wandering Hit by Ex Bar Head," November 19, 1948.

[125]Robert J Sickels, *Race, Marriage and the Law,* 1972, 112.

[126]*San Gabriel Sun,* "The Vorpal Sword," November 4, 1948.

[127]Spikard, *Mixed Blood,* 48, 70.

[128]Ruth Cavan, *The American Family* (New York, 1953), 244.

[129]Comment, *University of Virginia Law Review* 49: 1421, 1421 (1963).

[130]*Ibid.,* at 1422.

lutionary decision."[131] A note in the *Stanford Law Review* also discussed the
case approvingly.[132] However, on the whole, the initial scholarly response to
Perez was sparse and muted.

Perez had little effect on the U.S. Supreme Court, which passed up several
opportunities to rule on antimiscegenation statutes after *Perez*. In 1954, shortly
after the Supreme Court decided *Brown v. Board of Education,* it refused to hear
Jackson v. Alabama, a case in which the constitutionality of Alabama's antimiscegenation statute had been upheld by lower courts.[133] In 1956 the Court again
declined to take up the question of the constitutionality of an antimiscegenation
statute when it remanded *Naim v. Naim* for clarification of the record and subse-
quently ruled that the case lacked a federal question.[134] Not until the 1964 case
of *McLaughlin v. Florida,* which involved a challenge to a statute criminalizing
interracial cohabitation, did the Court move toward ruling on miscegenation.[135]
In *McLaughlin* the Court held that the statute violated the Equal Protection
Clause of the Constitution because it constituted arbitrary racial discrimination.
When the U.S. Supreme Court finally struck down Virginia's antimiscegenation
statute in *Loving v. Virginia* in 1967, the Court's opinion mentioned *Perez* only
once, deep in a footnote. *Loving* did not discuss *Perez* at all, except to recognize
that it marked the first and only instance in which a state court ruled that an antimiscegenation statute violated the Equal Protection Clause.[136] Much like Justice
Carter's opinion in *Perez,* Chief Justice Warren's opinion in *Loving* rested primarily on the broad principle of racial equality. Not only did Warren rely little
on *Perez* as precedent, but his analysis of the legal questions in *Loving* differed
substantially from Traynor's rationalistic analysis in *Perez*.

In the period separating *Perez* from *Loving* 14 states repealed their antimiscegenation statutes by legislative action. However, no state court struck down an
antimiscegenation statute during that time, strongly suggesting that *Perez* had
little or no impact outside of California.[137] Twelve state Supreme Courts upheld

---

[131]Case Note, *California Law Review* 37:122 (1949).

[132]Case Note, "Statutory Bar on Interracial Marriage Invalidated by 14th Amendment," *Stanford Law Review* 1:289 (1949).

[133]Jackson v. Alabama, 348 U.S. 888 (1954). This, despite the way in which the
Cold War confrontation intensified political pressures domestically and inspired many
judges to believe, as Chief Justice Earl Warren stated in 1954, that "The American system is on trial" and that advancement of civil rights would enhance security against international communism. (Mary L. Dudziak, *Cold War Civil Rights: Race and The Image of
American Democracy* (Princeton, 2000), 105–06).

[134]Naim v. Naim, 350 U.S. 891, 985 (1956).

[135]McLaughlin v. Florida, 379 U.S. 184 (1964).

[136]*Ibid.,* footnote 5.

[137]Sickels, *Race, Marriage and the Law,* 52.

the antimiscegenation statutes of their states.[138] All but one of these cases came before *Perez,* and the one case that came after *Perez* left the Virginia antimiscegenation statute in place.[139] Only three state Supreme Court decisions between *Perez* and *Loving* cited *Perez,* and then only to reject its holding.[140] The primary attack on these laws took place in the state legislatures, not in the courts.

It is possible that *Perez* prepared the way for legislative repeal of antimiscegenation statutes in some states, but this seems unlikely. During the 10 years after *Perez,* five states repealed their antimiscegenation statutes. In 1957 the southern and border states, along with Arizona, Colorado, Delaware, Idaho, Indiana, Nebraska, Nevada, Oklahoma, Utah, and Wyoming retained statutory prohibitions against miscegenation.[141] During the next 10 years another nine states repealed their antimiscegenation statutes by legislative action. By 1967 only the southern states and Delaware retained their antimiscegenation statutes. Political opposition to antimiscegenation statutes in the state legislatures probably had more to do with the civil rights movement than *Perez.* Although growing popular antipathy toward racism weakened support for antimiscegenation laws, mixed marriages remained a powerful taboo even after *Loving.*

Conclusion

Traynor's activism in *Perez* seems less audacious in hindsight because the values he expressed in his opinion have gained more widespread acceptance. His thinking about the role of the courts in promoting racial equality was, however, far ahead of its time. He thought critically about race relations, instead of seeing *Perez* only in terms of the narrow legal questions it presented. It is, therefore, ironic that his decision focused on the narrow legal question presented by the case—whether California's antimiscegenation law lacked a rational basis. It is

---

[138]Andrew Weinberger, "A Reappraisal of the Constitutionality of Miscegenation Statutes," *Cornell Law Quarterly* 42:208, 209 (1957).

[139]Naim v. Naim, 197 Va. 80 (1955).

[140]Only four cases after *Loving* cited *Perez.* None of these cases involved an antimiscegenation statute. In two decisions by the Alaska Supreme Court the majority cited *Perez* for the proposition that it "should not stand idly and passively, waiting for constitutional direction from the highest court of the land. Instead we should be moving concurrently to develop and expand the principles embedded in our constitutional law." Baker v. City of Fairbanks, 471 Pac.2d 386, 402 (1970); Roberts v. State, 458 Pac.2d 340 (1969). The Hawaii Supreme Court cited *Perez* twice, once in a case involving the denial of a marriage license to a same sex couple (Baehr v. Lewin, 852 Pac.2d 44 [1993]) and earlier for the general proposition that children of mixed marriages are not inferior (Almeida v. Correa, 465 Pac.2d 564 [1970]).

[141]Weinberger, "A Reappraisal of the Constitutionality of Miscegenation Statutes," 208, 208.

also paradoxical that Traynor used such a conventional method of analysis to reach such innovative results. Traynor was confident that modern science had exposed the fallacies underlying the antimiscegenation statute and that reasonable minds would concur in his judgment. *Perez* did not, however, provide impetus for lawyers and judges of a like mind. Instead, the legal community reacted to *Perez* with indifference. The absence of other cases following *Perez* demonstrated the persistent power of legal orthodoxy.

CHAPTER THREE

DeBurgh v. DeBurgh and the Public Interest in Family Life

A dominant characteristic of California family law in the early 1950s was its attachment to traditional conceptions of the role of women. Family law rested on the assumption that a woman's economic role was primarily as a worker in her own home—cleaning the house, caring for children, and preparing food and clothing. By the early 1950s, however, many women no longer performed traditional women's roles. A breach between family law, rooted in traditional assumptions about women's roles, and the changing realities of family life placed new pressures on lawmakers. Commentators have called the changes in family law during the twentieth century a "revolution in public philosophy."[1] As the ideal of family life changed in the post-New Deal era, lawmakers adapted the law to accommodate it.

The 1952 divorce case of *DeBurgh v. DeBurgh* brought before the California Supreme Court a legal question that could have been resolved easily by precedent, if the precedent had not conflicted with the justices' values and perception of societal realities.[2] The case arose out of an abusive relationship between Daisey DeBurgh and her husband Albert. Daisey and Albert moved to California in 1944 and lived together in Manhattan Beach before their marriage in 1946. Albert was a drinker who occasionally hit Daisey and bragged of his

---

[1]Steven Mintz and Susan Kellogg, *Domestic Revolutions: A Social History of American Family Life* (New York, 1988), 129.

[2]DeBurgh v. DeBurgh, 39 Cal.2d 858 (1952).

extramarital affairs. Several days before their separation in 1949, Daisey told Albert's business associates that Albert had had homosexual relations with three men. She also told Albert's business partner that Albert had defrauded her brother and bribed government officials.

Daisey sued for divorce and requested a restraining order against Albert. In response, Albert sued her for divorce as well. Each claimed the other had been guilty of "extreme cruelty" toward the other. The law permitted the court to grant a divorce only against a spouse deemed guilty of marital misconduct, and the court could only grant a divorce to a spouse deemed blameless. Under the legal doctrine of recrimination the court could not grant a divorce if both husband and wife had committed unprovoked marital misconduct.

As in all divorce cases, a judge tried *DeBurgh* without a jury. The trial lasted a day and a half. Trial judge Julius Patrosso pressured the lawyers to finish the case quickly, and his rulings from the bench indicated his impatience with both parties.[3] Albert DeBurgh's attorney, Donald Armstrong, attempted to portray his client as an upstanding businessman. Armstrong called several business associates to testify that they had not observed any homosexual behavior from Albert. Armstrong also told Judge Patrosso that he would call former judge John Shidler, who had previously represented Albert, to testify that Albert was not gay. (Armstrong ultimately did not call Shidler as a witness.) Theoretically this evidence merely refuted Daisey's claims of Albert's homosexual liaisons. Armstrong's broader strategy was to focus Judge Patrosso's attention on Daisey's apparently unfounded accusation and to bolster Albert's reputation. Armstrong carried more weight with Judge Patrosso than Daisey's lawyer, Jerry Rolston. Patrosso appeared to know and respect Armstrong. When he ruled on the case after the lawyers' closing arguments he referred to Armstrong as "having been thirty-five years in the practice of law and having had some experience in types of human conduct and domestic troubles."[4] Patrosso summarily refused to grant Rolston's request for financial support for Daisey and interrupted Rolston abruptly when he made the request.

Judge Patrosso ruled that both Albert and Daisey were at fault for the breakdown of their marriage, calling their marriage "a failure from the start."[5] Over Rolston's objection, Armstrong succeeded in bringing out evidence that Albert and Daisey had lived together out of wedlock. In his ruling from the bench at the end of the trial, the judge attributed the failure of the marriage to this fact. He believed that this living arrangement created a lack of trust that ul-

---

[3]The following description of the trial is drawn from the Reporter's Transcript on Appeal, Vols. I–II, May 23, 1951, DeBurgh Court File, California State Archives.

[4]DeBurgh Court File, Reporter's Transcript on Appeal, Vol. II, 394–95.

[5]*Ibid.*, 395.

timately destroyed the marriage. Under the doctrine of recrimination he refused
to grant a divorce to either Daisey or Albert. Daisey was the clear loser, and her
attorney moved for a new trial. When Judge Patrosso denied that request, Daisey
appealed the case.

Divorce *De Jure* and *De Facto*

California's scheme of divorce law had a long history. Barbara Armstrong, the
first tenured female professor at a major American law school and a close friend
and Boalt Hall colleague of Roger Traynor, traced the origins of California's
divorce statutes to English ecclesiastical courts.[6] California's Civil Code, enacted in 1872, incorporated the basic structures of English ecclesiastical law.
Under the Civil Code, married couples could not obtain divorces without proving to the court that one spouse had committed one of the types of marital misconduct recognized by law. The Civil Code listed six grounds for divorce: adultery, extreme cruelty (defined as "the wrongful infliction of grievous bodily
injury, or grievous mental suffering"), willful desertion, willful neglect, habitual
intemperance, and conviction of a felony. The 1872 code also established defenses to a divorce action: connivance, collusion, condonation, or lapse of time.
California divorce law remained almost entirely unchanged until 1941 when the
legislature added incurable insanity as grounds for divorce.[7]

The doctrine of recrimination also traced its lineage to the English ecclesiastical courts. The ecclesiastical courts developed the doctrine in accordance with
the underlying principle of divorce law that divorce could not be permitted
unless one and only one spouse was at fault for the marital breakdown. The
eighteenth-century ecclesiastical court opinion *Beeby v. Beeby* explained the
policy behind the doctrine. Denying divorce to both parties would enable the
spouses to "find sources of mutual forgiveness in the humiliation of mutual
guilt."[8] By the early 1950s, the general pattern of English divorce law had been
long established in California, and most other states had a longstanding scheme
of divorce law similar to California's.[9]

Despite its strictness in principle California divorce law did not constrain irreconcilable spouses. As Barbara Armstrong noted in 1953, "[d]ivorce in legal

---

[6]*Ibid.*, 225.

[7]Barbara Armstrong, *California Family Law: Persons and Domestic Relations, The
Community Property System,* Vol. I (San Francisco, 1953), 130.

[8]Beeby v. Beeby, 1 Hagg. Ecc. 789, 790 (1799); Herma Hill Kay, "A Family Court:
The California Proposal," *California Law Review* 56:1205, 1213–14 (1968).

[9]Armstrong, *California Family Law,* Vol. I, 128.

theory is widely separated from divorce in practical fact."[10] Divorce law and practice diverged well before the 1950s. The following 1945 testimonial of senior Los Angeles County Superior Court Judge Swain suggested a longstanding practice of granting divorces to irreconcilable spouses:

> When I began the practice of law there were such stalwarts on the bench . . . who did not grant divorce decrees on the ground of cruelty unless serious misconduct of the defendant was proven. Since that time an attitude has grown up of "what is the use of denying a default decree, the parties know best, if they can't get along they are better off divorced."[11]

In 1953 over 90 percent of divorces resulted from a collusive agreement between spouses.[12] The spouses would agree that one of them would allege grounds for divorce, usually mental cruelty, and the other would not contest the divorce action. Judges merely ratified the spouses' decision. Boalt Hall professor Herma Hill Kay, a family law expert who clerked for Traynor in 1959 and 1960, described divorce proceedings of the time as "a well-established legal charade with a script written by divorce lawyers and acted out by the parties to permit the judge to achieve a result permissible by the letter of the law but forbidden by its spirit."[13] A 1953 sociology textbook echoed the view of most commentators on family law when it described divorce proceedings as "a farce."[14] By the 1950s, one of the most prominent features of divorce law, the notion of the blameless spouse, came to be treated by the courts as a fiction or, at best, an irrelevancy.

The Setting for Reform:
Divorce and the Changing Status of Women

During the 1940s, fifties, and sixties, most legal commentators on divorce considered divorce an evil and an important national problem. Los Angeles County Superior Court Presiding Judge Louis Burke referred to "the breakup of homes by divorce" as a "national tragedy."[15] "Divorce," he wrote, "is a disease, and in

---

[10]*Ibid.*, 125.

[11]Superior Court Judge Swain, "Default Divorce," *Los Angeles Bar Bulletin,* Vol. 21, No. 2 (October 1945): 53.

[12]Armstrong, *California Family Law,* 124.

[13]Kay, "A Family Court," 1205, 1217.

[14]Cavan, *The American Family,* 490.

[15]Presiding Judge Louis Burke, Los Angeles Superior Court, "Problems of Court Administration: Metropolitan Court," *Journal of the State Bar* 43:928, 940 (1959).

America it has reached epidemic proportions.[16] San Mateo County Superior Court Judge Frank Blum echoed this view in 1966 when he wrote that divorce is a "disease which has reached epidemic proportions . . . nationally."[17]

Divorce statistics provided fodder for alarmists. At the turn of the century the United States had the highest divorce rate in the world.[18] According to the U.S. Public Health Service *Monthly Vital Statistics Report,* the annual divorce rate then increased between 1900 and 1940 from 4 to 8.8 per 1,000 married women age 15 or older.[19] The divorce rate increased dramatically during World War II and peaked in 1946 at almost 17.8 per 1,000.[20] After the war, the divorce rate fell to 10–11 per 1,000 and remained there through the 1950s.[21]

By some measures, social acceptance of divorce grew after World War II along with the divorce rate. One of the strongest indications of the increasing acceptance of divorce was the trend among many religious denominations toward a liberalized position on divorce. Although the Catholic Church consistently resisted this trend, the Episcopal, Methodist, Lutheran, and Northern and Southern Presbyterian churches loosened their policies regarding the treatment of people seeking divorce and divorcees seeking to remarry.[22] Legislative reform of divorce statutes also suggested changing attitudes toward divorce. Some states that followed the recrimination doctrine weakened the doctrine by making it discretionary, by adding grounds for divorce, such as "incompatibility," or instituting a policy of "comparative rectitude."[23]

Nonetheless, opinion surveys on the subject of divorce did not support a relaxation of the legal requirements for divorce. To the contrary, various opinion polls showed widespread disapproval of divorce. When asked, "Should divorces be easier to obtain in your state?" 77 percent of Californians surveyed answered "no" in 1936. Those surveyed in the other states shared that sentiment 77 percent

---

[16]*Ibid.*

[17]Judge Frank Blum, Superior Court Judge, San Mateo County, "Conciliation Courts: Instruments of Peace," *Journal of the State Bar* 41:33, 43 (1966).

[18]Mintz and Kellogg, *Domestic Revolutions,* 109.

[19]National Office of Vital Statistics, "Summary of Marriage and Divorce Statistics: United States 1950," *Vital Statistics Special Report,* Volume 37, No. 3 (October 29, 1952), 52.

[20]*Ibid.*

[21]*Ibid.;* Mintz and Kellogg, *Domestic Revolutions,* 179.

[22]Nelson Manfred Blake, *The Road to Reno: A History of Divorce in the United States* (New York, 1962), 229–31.

[23]George Basye, "Retreat from Recrimination," *California Law Review* 41:320, 321 (1953). Under the comparative rectitude doctrine a spouse, who was not blameless, could obtain a divorce if the fault of the other spouse were greater than his or her own.

of the time.[24] In 1937, *Fortune* magazine conducted a poll on the question "Do you think there should be easy divorce laws so that it would not be so expensive and troublesome to dissolve an unhappy marriage?" Fifty-four percent said "no," 28 percent said "yes," and 11 percent said, "no divorce should be allowed."[25] In 1945 the American Institute of Public Opinion conducted a poll that asked, "Do you think the divorce laws in this state now are too strict or not strict enough?" Only nine percent of the national sample surveyed thought divorce laws were "too strict," 35 percent thought they were "not strict enough," 31 percent answered "about right," and 25 percent said they were "undecided."[26]

Fundamental changes in the status of women contributed to high divorce rates after World War II, despite widespread disapproval of divorce. Women became increasingly economically independent. The role of the modern housewife as consumer and provider clashed with the traditional roles of women as mothers and wives. The availability of consumer products eliminated the need for much home production and freed women from some of their traditional, time-consuming labors. At the same time, the movement of women into work places outside the home removed them from the place where mothering traditionally occurred. As women took jobs outside the home they increasingly interacted with men in the work place, changing the social mores that had isolated them. Their earnings helped support their families financially, but at the same time undermined the traditional dynamics of family life, in which the husband was the sole breadwinner.

The Depression had already diminished the stature of many husbands as breadwinners for their families. The economic and social pressures of the Depression encouraged family disintegration, and many families did not survive the Depression intact. The number of children placed in custodial institutions increased 50 percent during the first two years of the Depression.[27] The Depression may well have increased social condemnation of working mothers.[28] A 1938 poll showed that over 80 percent of Americans surveyed strongly opposed the employment outside the home of married women.[29] Many firms laid off married women workers to save men's ("head of the family") jobs. Most Americans

---

[24]Clifford Kirkpatrick, *The Family as Process and Institution* (New York, 1955), 538–39, citing the A.I.P.O. Survey of April 1936.

[25]As quoted in *Ibid.* at 513.

[26]As quoted in *Ibid.* at 513.

[27]Mintz and Kellogg, *Domestic Revolutions,* 136.

[28]Lois Scharf, *To Work and To Wed: Female Employment, Feminism, and the Great Depression* (Westport, Connecticut, 1980), 43.

[29]William Chafe, *The American Woman: Her Changing Social Economic and Political Roles, 1920–1970* (New York, 1972), 148.

still believed that the primary role of married women was as wives and mothers, but, by eroding traditional gender roles, the Depression had begun to undermine societal resistance to women in the workforce.

The rate of female employment increased dramatically during World War II.[30] Over six million women went to work outside their homes during the war, increasing the number of women workers by half.[31] The war also changed the profile of the female workforce.[32] Before the war the typical working woman was young and single. Three-fourths of the new, women workers were married; the number of married women who worked doubled.[33] By the end of the war the typical female worker was married and over 40. Attitudes toward married women in the workforce changed as well. A 1942 poll showed that 60 percent of those surveyed believed women should be employed in war industries.[34] The war helped married women gain acceptance in the workplace.

Like the Depression, the war disrupted family life. Sixteen million people moved into the military, and another 15 million civilians migrated to find work in the war industries.[35] The itinerancy of family life during the war broke networks of family ties, as relatives separated and lost touch with communities where they had roots. This unprecedented mobility helped break down patterns of female domesticity.

After the war, although half of the women in the workforce quit or lost their jobs,[36] important demographic factors continued to increase the economic independence of women. They were becoming better educated; by 1940 women received over 40 percent of the bachelor and professional degrees.[37] The workplace became more attractive to women as real wages for work outside the home increased, and workplace regulations—particularly the eight-hour day—made it easier for women to earn a wage while managing traditional domestic duties. Married white women moved into the labor market more quickly in the 1950s than in any decade before or since, increasing their work rate from 17 percent to

---

[30]See Mintz and Kellogg, *Domestic Revolutions,* 94.

[31]Chafe, *The American Woman,* 135; Mintz and Kellogg, *Domestic Revolutions,* 95.

[32]Chafe, *The American Woman,* 144.

[33]*Ibid.*

[34]*Ibid.,* 148.

[35]Mintz and Kellogg, *Domestic Revolutions,* 155.

[36]*Ibid.,* 95.

[37]*Ibid.,* 91.

30 percent.[38] The increasing economic independence of women affected their outlook toward marriage and their attitudes toward divorce.

By the 1950s, expectations of marriage had been in the process of change for decades. The increasing economic independence of women merely accelerated a growing inclination to marry for sentimental rather than other, more traditional reasons.[39] As a 1953 sociology textbook unequivocally stated, "In our culture love is regarded as the primary motive for marriage."[40] For a growing number of middle-class couples marriage was supposed to provide emotional fulfillment, romance, and sexual satisfaction.[41] According to the modern ideal of the "companionate marriage," spouses would be friends and lovers. Marriages endured not because of social and economic pressure or religious strictures, but because of mutual affection.

The group of women who took the greatest strides toward economic independence during the 1950s also filed for divorce most often. They were white, native born, in their twenties or early thirties, and middle class.[42] Los Angeles County Superior Court Judge William Palmer studied Los Angeles divorce cases in 1952 and found that wives filed 682 of 882 divorce cases in his court.[43] Three quarters of these women were under 40, most were white, and 42 percent claimed community property. They generally cited cruelty as the grounds for divorce. Stanley Mosk's study of Los Angeles County divorces in 1954 yielded similar results.[44] According to Mosk, the typical plaintiff in a divorce action was a white female. The average age of women filing for divorce was 34, and there was community property in 54 percent of the cases.

The couples who brought divorce actions persuaded the courts to adopt new practical standards for divorce. California divorce law—as it actually functioned—reflected a shift toward the ideal of "companionate marriage." Allegations of adultery, once the most common grounds for divorce, became less fre-

---

[38]Lynn Y. Winer, *From Working Girl to Working Mother: The Female Labor Force in the United States, 1820–1980* (Chapel Hill, North Carolina, 1985); Mintz and Kellogg, *Domestic Revolutions,* 89.

[39]See Kirkpatrick, *The Family as Process and Institution.*

[40]Cavan, *The American Family,* 397.

[41]Kirkpatrick, *The Family as Process and Institution,* 135; Edward Shorter, *The Making of the Modern Family* (New York, 1975).

[42]Scharf, *To Work and To Wed,* 107.

[43]Hon. William J. Palmer, Superior Court Los Angeles County, "Divorce Facts and Fiction," *The Legal Eagle,* A Bulletin for Bench and Bar of the Bay Counties, Vol. I, No. 10 (1952), 3.

[44]Stanley Mosk, "Ingredients of the Divorce Test Tube," *Los Angeles Bar Bulletin,* Vol. 29, No. 6 (March, 1954), 177–79.

quent.[45] The use of extreme cruelty—which included intentional infliction of emotional suffering—as a grounds for divorce, increased dramatically.[46] The ideal of "companionate marriage" raised the standards for marital conduct, making the intentional infliction of emotional suffering behavior that the courts did not require either spouse to tolerate. Traynor detected some movement in California case law away from an analysis based on fault and toward an analysis based on marital breakdown. "We cannot ignore the important social considerations which make it contrary to public policy to insist on the maintenance of a union which has utterly broken down," Traynor wrote in *DeBurgh,* quoting from two recent California Supreme Court cases.[47] Through a growing number of divorce cases, the courts adopted higher standards for marriage, despite widespread opposition to easy divorce.

In the modern, nuclear family the mutual affection of family members was the mainstay of family life. The social and religious pressures that had buttressed the family lost some of their force. During the 1950s, sociologists frequently observed that the family had turned inward and become increasingly autonomous from the surrounding community.[48] These changes in family life created new demands on the law of marriage and divorce.

The loosely defined Family Life Movement, composed of academics, practitioners, and organizations such as the National Council on Family Relations (NCFR) coalesced in response to a felt need for new forms of support for the increasingly isolated and insular nuclear family. In 1948 the movement converged at the National Conference on Family Life in Washington, D.C. With the support of the NCFR and input from a wide variety of professional organizations, including the American Bar Association, it advocated a divorce scheme that emphasized family reconciliation through counseling.

Central to the reform proposals of the Family Life Movement was the family court. Family court would subsume jurisdiction over divorce, juvenile dependency, child custody, and adoption. It would operate on a therapeutic model, relying heavily on professional family counselors. Its goal would be family reconciliation. Even before the war, California had begun experimenting with specialized family courts—called Courts of Conciliation—that emphasized family counseling and reconciliation. Although no other county beside Los Angeles

[45]Paul Bohannan, ed., *Divorce and After* (Garden City, New York, 1970), 16.

[46]*Ibid.,* 19; Also see Public Health Service, National Center for Health Statistics, Divorce Statistics Analysis 1963, Series 21, No 13 (October, 1967) Table 7.

[47]DeBurgh, 39 Cal.2d 870, quoting Hill v. Hill, 23 Cal.2d 82, 93 (1943); and Weil v. Weil, 37 Cal.2d 770, 783–84 (1951).

[48]See e.g., Kirkpatrick, *The Family as Process and Institution;* Cavan, *The American Family;* and Ernest Burgess and Harvey Locke, *The Family: From Institution to Companionship,* 2d ed. (New York, 1950).

established a Court of Conciliation, Los Angeles judges proclaimed theirs a great success. The legal unorthodoxy of the Court of Conciliation drew criticism from several legal commentators, but it helped establish California's reputation for innovative family law reform.

Traynor did not mention family courts in *DeBurgh,* but he was surely well aware of them. By the time Traynor wrote his opinion in *DeBurgh,* substantial support existed within the legal community for a shift in the focus of divorce law from fault to marital breakdown. One of the legal profession's most prominent critics of fault-based divorce was Traynor's close friend Professor Barbara Armstrong. She influenced Traynor's thinking on family law more than any other advisor. In 1919, at the age of 29, Armstrong became the first woman law professor in the country when she joined the Boalt faculty.[49] Traynor was a student of hers at Boalt, and the two maintained a close friendship after that. Armstrong authored the leading 1950s legal treatise on California family law, and Traynor kept it on his desk.[50] In keeping with her belief that the law should permit women to gain their independence from failed marriages, Armstrong advocated a shift away from fault-based divorce. Traynor recognized that within the legal profession there was widespread skepticism about the wisdom of recrimination. "Few rules of law," he wrote in *DeBurgh,* "have been more widely condemned by the legal profession."[51] In 1950 the American Bar Association had helped form the Interprofessional Commission on Marriage and Divorce Laws, which reported that family stability suffered from a fault-based scheme of divorce law. Traynor cited in his opinion the 1948 report to the American Bar Association of the National Conference on Family Life, which advocated the outright abolition of recrimination, along with the adoption of a therapeutic model for family law.[52] He agreed with reform advocates that marital breakdown—and not divorce—was the underlying social ill that family law should address. Divorce proceedings should focus, therefore, on marital breakdown rather than fault.

The Dynamics of Divorce Cases

In 1950s divorce cases, husbands were often shown to have exercised physical as well as economic power over their wives. Although divorce had come to be

---

[49]Beth Hollenberg, "Full of Zoom: Barbara Nachtrieb Armstrong, First Woman Professor of Law" (Paper for Professor Barbara Babcock, Stanford, 1997), 3.

[50]Interview with Dean Herma Hill Kay by Ben Field, August 15, 1997.

[51]DeBurgh, 39 Cal.2d at 870.

[52]*Ibid.,* 870.

seen as "easy," and legal commentators bemoaned the scripted "two slaps" re-counted by many wives in divorce proceedings, actual domestic violence was not unusual. As Stanley Mosk commented in 1954,

> my experience is that gross cruelty is the rule, rather than the exception and that actual physical assaults and violence occur in a startling number of cases. Of the 506 [cases] I analyzed, there was testimony of violence of some nature in 210, or approximately 41 percent of the actions. . . . No attempt was made to distinguish the extent of the violence, and it varied from mere slapping to se-vere beatings resulting in broken bones. But the fact that so many persons re-sort to force in their domestic life is revealing and disturbing.[53]

DeBurgh exemplified the sort of physical abuse that often underlay divorce cases. Daisey DeBurgh testified about both emotional and physical abuse. She told the court that Albert had punched her in the face on several occasions over the course of years, and her lawyer called other witnesses at trial to corroborate her account of the beatings. In his decision, Traynor made note of the evidence that after one severe beating Daisey attempted suicide with sleeping pills. As with other disintegrating marriages, Albert apparently used physical force to control the dynamics of home life.

Like most husbands in divorce cases, Albert had not only a physical advan-tage, but an economic advantage over his wife. Although most divorces in 1952 were uncontested, divorcing spouses did fight over the distribution of marital property, support payments, child custody, and visitation rights. Divorcing spouses generally resolved these disputes out of court.[54] However, their negotia-tions certainly reflected their assessments of how the courts would view their claims. A court's assessment of fault could affect the distribution of a married couple's property and the court's determination of marital support. In 1952 the California Civil Code stated that the court could require only the spouse deemed to be at fault to pay alimony and child support.[55] The Civil Code generally gave husbands and wives equal interests in community property.[56] However, a spouse granted a divorce on grounds of cruelty or adultery could expect to receive more than half of the community property.[57] The spouse found to be solely at fault in a contested divorce could expect to be penalized in the determination of support

---

[53]Stanley Mosk, "Ingredients of the Divorce Test Tube," *Los Angeles Bar Bulletin,* Vol. 29, No. 6, 164.

[54]Max Rheinstein, *Marriage Stability, Divorce, and the Law* (Chicago, 1972), 247.

[55]California Civil Code, section 139 (1952).

[56]California Civil Code, section 161a. (1952).

[57]See Tipton v. Tipton, 209 Cal.443 (1930); Eslinger, 47 Cal.62 (1873); California Civil Code, section 146(1).

and the distribution of community property. California divorce law therefore created an incentive for recrimination claims in contested divorce suits.

The threat of a recrimination allegation influenced financial negotiations between divorcing spouses. It generally helped husbands who had committed marital misconduct avoid economic loss. The husband's recrimination allegation created the possibility that the wife might be found solely at fault and therefore receive no alimony or child support. If the court found both spouses to be at fault, the husband, who generally held the economic power in the household, could dictate the terms of any divorce. Even a wife with a strong case for divorce would discount her demands for marital property and support payments because of the risk that a recrimination claim would succeed.

The *DeBurgh* case was typical in this way. Daisey DeBurgh did not work outside the home and therefore was economically dependent on Albert, who earned a substantial income. Albert, like all husbands in California divorce cases, controlled all the marital assets because the state's Civil Code entrusted marital assets to husbands, enabling them to use those assets as they saw fit without informing their spouses.[58] As the code stated, "The husband is the head of the family. He may choose any reasonable place or mode of living, and the wife must conform thereto."[59] The husband had the sole power to manage community property, except for the wife's earnings.[60] A married woman who did not work outside the home and who had no separate property could not obtain credit in her own name without her husband's consent. A wife had no clear legal remedies available to her during the marriage to prevent her husband's mismanagement of the property and no clear right even to know the extent or location of the community assets. Although obligated to support Daisey, Albert had great leeway to spend their assets as he saw fit.

Daisey, like all wives in California divorce cases, found herself in a financially powerless position, without control of the marital assets and with limited information about what or where they were. As commentators cited by Traynor in his opinion had pointed out, husbands used the recrimination doctrine to blackmail their wives; the threat of continued marriage, even after marital breakdown, made palatable what otherwise might have seemed an unfair marital property distribution and alimony determination.[61] Daisey, who wanted the divorce more than Albert did, faced two unattractive options. She could risk a court's finding that the recrimination doctrine applied, which would perpetuate

---

[58]California Civil Code, sections 161a, 172, 172a (1952).

[59]California Civil Code, section 5101 (1952).

[60]California Civil Code, sections 5105 and 5127 (1952).

[61]John Bradway, "The Myth of the Innocent Spouse," *Tulane Law Review* 11:377 (1937).

her marriage to a physically abusive partner who controlled all the marital assets, or she could bargain away some of her financial interests in order to gain Albert's acquiescence to a divorce.

When Traynor wrote his opinion in *DeBurgh,* the economic and physical power of husbands over wives had been long taken for granted by judges in divorce cases. If judges attempted to redress this imbalance of power, they did so through the exercise of their discretion to determine property allocations and support payments. They did not alter the rules that created the imbalance of power. As a result, the legal precedents that buttressed the husband's domestic dominance remained in use at the time of *DeBurgh.*

The Departure from Precedent

Until *DeBurgh,* California courts had interpreted the recrimination doctrine in a way Traynor referred to as "mechanical."[62] *Conant v. Conant,* decided in 1858, 14 years before the legislature codified the recrimination doctrine in Civil Code section 122, held that courts could grant a divorce only to a spouse deemed blameless.[63] Mrs. Conant sued for divorce on the grounds that her husband had committed adultery. He defended himself on the grounds that she had deserted him one year prior to his adultery. The California Supreme Court refused to grant a divorce because both spouses had committed misconduct. Several cases interpreted *Conant* to mean that if both spouses committed any misconduct sufficient to justify divorce neither spouse could obtain a divorce.[64]

This "mechanical" application of the recrimination doctrine was so deeply ingrained that Daisey DeBurgh's lawyers did not bother to argue against it. They made two other arguments instead. First, they argued that Albert provoked Daisey's misconduct: she accused him of homosexuality and dishonesty only in response to beatings and other misconduct by him. Since provocation and recrimination were mutually exclusive defenses to a divorce action, Albert could not prevent Daisey from getting a divorce if he had provoked her marital misconduct. Second, Daisey's lawyers argued that the court could award support to Daisey, who had separated from Albert, even though the court denied her a divorce. Nowhere in their written arguments to the court did Daisey's lawyers argue for reform of the recrimination doctrine.

---

[62]DeBurgh, 39 Cal.2d at 870.

[63]Conant v. Conant, 10 Cal. 249 (1858).

[64]Sweazey v. Sweazey, 126 Cal. 123 (1899); Mattson v. Mattson, 181 Cal. 44 (1919).

Traynor went out of his way to address problems he saw with the recrimination doctrine. Early in his decision he agreed with Daisey DeBurgh's fundamental contention that Albert provoked her misconduct. "[T]he evidence would support the finding that defendant's [Albert's] cruelty provoked the accusations made by the plaintiff [Daisey]," Traynor wrote.[65] He could have stopped his analysis there or chosen the even more cautious route taken by Justice Edmonds in his concurring opinion. Edmonds sought to send the case back to the trial court for a determination of whether Albert provoked Daisey's misconduct. Instead, Traynor broke with precedent first by nullifying the doctrine of recrimination and then by opening the possibility that both spouses could be awarded a divorce.

Traynor made three interrelated arguments against the recrimination doctrine. The first argument was based on a statutory interpretation of Civil Code section 122. The second was based on the history of recrimination. The third and most important was based on public policy. Neither Daisey's nor Albert's lawyers had advanced any of these arguments, though Daisey DeBurgh's attorneys presumably felt duty bound to make any legal argument they thought would help their client. They did not ask the Court to reform the recrimination doctrine, no doubt because they considered the doctrine settled. Traynor's willingness to address issues not raised by the parties revealed his desire to attack the recrimination doctrine.

The reaction of some of Traynor's brethren to his opinion showed that, like the attorneys, they considered the recrimination doctrine settled. Justices Edmonds, Spence, and Shenk, who agreed with Traynor's result, disagreed with his interpretation of the recrimination statute. They agreed with Traynor that the trial judge seemed to have incorrectly denied Daisey's divorce action after finding that Albert provoked her misconduct, but they saw no grounds for overruling prior case law. According to Traynor, the language of Civil Code section 122, which codified a definition of the recrimination doctrine, conflicted with the interpretation of the doctrine arising from *Conant*. Civil Code section 111 provided that "Divorces must be denied upon a showing of . . . recrimination." Civil Code section 122 defined recrimination as "a showing by the defendant of any cause of divorce against the plaintiff, in bar of the plaintiff's cause of divorce."[66] Traynor contended that divorce should not be denied to all spouses whose conduct constituted a cause of divorce, only those spouses whose misconduct was "in bar" of the other spouse's divorce suit. Why else would the legislature have inserted the "in bar" language, Traynor asked. The legislature could have simply

---

[65]DeBurgh, 39 Cal.2d at 862.
[66]California Civil Code, section 122 (1872).

required the denial of any divorce action by a spouse whose own conduct constituted grounds for divorce.

Justice Edmonds interpreted the language of section 122 to mean that "any
cause of divorce against the plaintiff" was a "bar to the plaintiff's cause of divorce."[67] Traynor's interpretation, Edmonds pointed out, ignored "the mandatory
'must' of section 111 and gave the court 'discretion' in determining whether to
grant a divorce where each party has shown a cause of divorce against the
other."[68] Both Edmonds and Shenk wrote in separate opinions that the text of
Civil Code 122 had been correctly interpreted over time, and they saw no acceptable reason to reinterpret it.

Traynor and Edmonds disagreed sharply over the legislative history of the
recrimination doctrine. Traynor claimed historical support for his statutory rein-
terpretation. According to him, *Conant*'s ruling that the court could grant a divorce only to a spouse deemed "beyond reproach" misinterpreted English ecclesiastical authority. Moreover, he argued, the legislature had rejected the rule of
ecclesiastical courts, which *Conant* claimed to adopt. The legislature, Traynor
asserted, never intended to make the blamelessness of one spouse a more important requirement for divorce than the "public interest in the institution of marriage" when it adopted the Civil Code in 1872.[69] Traynor defended what he saw
as the legislature's intent and opened the door for a discussion of public policy—his most forceful argument in favor of reform.

Justice Edmonds's opinion contains a substantial rebuttal of Traynor's historical argument. He argued that none of the cases cited by the commissioners
who drafted the Civil Code supported Traynor's interpretation of the recrimination statute. According to Edmonds, the Civil Code Commission adopted the
reasoning of *Conant*. By using "considerations of public policy . . . in effect, this
court repeals the statutory rule of recrimination," he wrote. "Only the embalmed
corpse of the doctrine is preserved."[70] Edmonds not only disagreed with
Traynor's historical and textual analysis; he found most of the opinion "unwarranted."[71] Traynor's ruling that both parties could be awarded divorce decrees
particularly galled Edmonds, who pointed out the absence of any legal authority
for such an interpretation of the recrimination doctrine.

Traynor favored the abolition of recrimination, but he felt he lacked
grounds to strike down the recrimination statute outright. As Edmonds noted, by
giving judges discretion to decide whether the misconduct of both spouses

---

[67] DeBurgh, 39 Cal.2d at 876.

[68] *Ibid.*, 875.

[69] *Ibid.*, 863.

[70] *Ibid.*, 880.

[71] *Ibid.*, 875.

barred either from divorce, Traynor did eliminate recrimination in effect, even though the statute remained on the books. His ultimate conclusions in *DeBurgh* changed divorce law with little if any support of precedent, and he, of course, knew it. "I did that [*DeBurgh*] based on my strong right arm," he told his law clerk, Herma Hill Kay.[72] As in other innovative Traynor decisions, Traynor's conclusions in *DeBurgh* relied primarily on his conception of the public interest involved.

The Public Interest in the Institution of Marriage

The heart of Traynor's opinion in *DeBurgh* was not his interpretation of statutory language, his discussion of the history of recrimination, or his analysis of legislative intent. Rather it was his public policy argument. Traynor referred 12 times in his opinion to "public interest," "public policy," and the interests of society. In response, Edmonds attacked Traynor for judicial legislation:

> This court should not usurp the legislative prerogative by the device of interpreting a statute which needs no interpretation, and which has been accepted without question for 80 years. If public policy no longer approves the doctrine of recrimination, then it is for the Legislature, and not for the court, to repeal the statute.[73]

Unlike Edmonds, Traynor did not place public policymaking and judicial decision making in separate compartments. Traynor insisted that judges had made policy-based decisions in the past and should continue to do so openly. For Traynor "considerations of policy" simply outweighed the precedent in support of the recrimination doctrine.[74] "Since the family is the core of our society, the law seeks to foster and preserve marriage," he wrote. "But when a marriage has failed and the family has ceased to be a unit, the purposes of family life are no longer served and divorce will be permitted."[75]

Traynor acknowledged growing concern about "the rising divorce rate."[76] He concluded, however, that the recrimination doctrine operated on the incorrect assumption that the courts' refusal to recognize marital breakdown could preserve marriages. The recrimination doctrine did not discourage divorce so much

---

[72]Interview with Herma Hill Kay by Ben Field, August 15, 1997.

[73]*Ibid.*, 882.

[74]*Ibid.*, 864.

[75]*Ibid.*, 864.

[76]*Ibid.*, 867.

as it exerted a "corrupting influence" on the institution of marriage.[77] Recrimination failed to achieve its goal of discouraging divorce because of its erroneous assumption that "technical marital fault" ought to be the focus of divorce law. Forcing irreconcilable spouses to remain married made "a mockery of marriage."[78] Nullifying the recrimination doctrine, on the other hand, would help preserve the institutional integrity of marriage.

Recognizing the "irremedial breakdown of the marriage" as the social problem underlying divorce, Traynor concluded that granting divorce to both spouses where both were at fault was good public policy.[79] Society had an interest in supporting the family both because of the family's role in society and because of its role in the lives of family members. Traynor drew on the traditional notion that the family helped ensure social stability. It "channels biological drives that might otherwise become socially destructive . . . [and] ensures the care and education of children in a stable environment."[80] Traynor also embraced the modern view that the family "nurtures and develops the individual initiative that distinguishes a free people."[81] The family served a public interest by encouraging individual growth within the private sphere of the home. The notion of the family as the foundation of a well-ordered society gave Traynor's argument the legitimacy of basic, accepted policy regarding the family as an institution.

Traynor believed a husband's physical or economic coercion of his wife subverted the public interest in the family as a haven for individual growth. Public interest did not require the preservation of the family if it meant ignoring this coercion. "[P]ublic policy," Traynor wrote, "was not served by forcing a wife, even if guilty, to return to a home where her life was in danger."[82] He realized that the physical power imbalance between spouses allowed abusive husbands to use recrimination to their advantage: "[T]he more unscrupulous partner may obtain substantial financial concessions as the price of remaining silent (and thus permitting an uncontested divorce action)."[83] A husband like Albert DeBurgh benefited financially in a divorce action from the threat of future domestic violence because the prospect of continued marriage was so unpleasant to his spouse.

---

[77] *Ibid.*, 869.

[78] *Ibid.*, 867.

[79] *Ibid.*, 872.

[80] *Ibid.*, 864.

[81] *Ibid.*

[82] *Ibid.*, 865.

[83] *Ibid.*, 869.

Traynor recognized the centrality of gender equality issues in divorce cases.[84] "[I]t is significant," he wrote, "that the application of a strict rule of recrimination does not operate with equal justice."[85] *DeBurgh* revealed Traynor's concern that husbands used their superior economic power under the law to gain an unfair advantage in divorce proceedings. Implicit in his conception of the public interest in marriage was the ideal of "companionate marriage." By nullifying the recrimination doctrine Traynor advanced that ideal and eliminated a rule that treated spouses unequally. Traynor's own experience of marriage involved the emotional and intellectual companionship of a person treated as an equal.[86] His wife Madeleine was an outspoken advisor on various legal issues. She went to law school herself in the late fifties. Traynor encouraged her interest in the law and, by all accounts, enjoyed the exchange of ideas with her. For him, the normative roles of husband and wife paralleled his experience of marriage.

Traynor's articulation of the public interest in marriage revealed his sensitivity to demands for greater individual freedom within the institution of marriage. However, as Herma Hill Kay and others, most notably feminist sociologist Lenore Weitzman, have pointed out, no-fault divorce had the unanticipated result of impoverishing many divorced women and their children.[87] It meant an equal distribution of community property between spouses. However, wives who had not worked outside the home had little earning power so the equal distribution of community property had an unequal financial impact. The advent of no-fault divorce triggered a new debate over the meaning of equality within marriage. Unlike the debate over no-fault divorce, this new debate was connected with the rise of feminism. "[T]he theme of equality between men and women assumed preeminence in California family law reform only after the adoption of the no-fault divorce law in 1970," according to Kay.[88] Implicit in Traynor's conception of marriage was the assumption that marriage was a partnership of equals. Efforts to achieve equality between divorcing spouses flowed from this basic premise.

---

[84]Dean Herma Hill Kay recalled from her time as a clerk for Traynor that this awareness of gender issues was rare for men of that time. Interview with Herma Hill Kay by Ben Field, August 15, 1997.

[85]*Ibid.*, 872.

[86]Impressions of Traynor's relationship with his wife were gleaned from several interviews with close friends and colleagues including Don Barrett, Herma Hill Kay, Adrian Kragen, and John Junker.

[87]Herma Hill Kay, "An Appraisal of California's No-Fault Divorce Law," *California Law Review* 75:291, 293 (1987); Lenore Weitzman, *The Divorce Revolution* (New York, 1985), 365–66.

[88]Kay, "An Appraisal of California's No-Fault Divorce Law," 291, 309.

The Impact of the *DeBurgh* Case

In an addendum to her treatise, *California Family Law,* Barbara Armstrong wrote of *DeBurgh,* "No single decision has done more for the integrity of the bar, the preservation of the sound morals of the community and the wholesome functioning of the equity powers inherent in our courts."[89] However, *DeBurgh* appears hardly to have entered the thinking of people outside of the legal community. A handful of newspapers printed articles about *DeBurgh,* but the decision generated little public reaction.

Newspaper coverage of *DeBurgh* did not encourage controversy. Several articles pointed out that only a 4–3 majority had voted to overturn the 80-year-old recrimination doctrine.[90] These articles did not create the impression that the case promoted easier divorce. Some of the reporting on the case even explained that recrimination was a "method frequently . . . used to block property settlements."[91] This recognition of the dynamics of divorce proceedings suggests an explanation for the lack of controversy surrounding *DeBurgh*. The case seemed to involve little more than the elimination of an anachronistic rule used by divorcing spouses to gain a financial advantage. To the extent that *DeBurgh* gained public attention at all, it was not seen as the harbinger of no-fault divorce, nor was it perceived as a threat to the institutions of marriage and family.

DeBurgh gained little scholarly attention outside the state. There were few law review citations to the case. Only a handful of law reviews outside California cited *DeBurgh* and then only in the 1960s as no-fault divorce reform gained attention.[92] At the time of the decision, only articles in California law journals recognized *DeBurgh* as an important departure from precedent. Even these articles emphasized that *DeBurgh* exemplified a general trend away from orthodoxy in divorce law. As one commentator in the *California Law Review* noted, the decision "was not quite so startling when viewed against the background of recent developments in California and elsewhere."[93]

Other states were already moving away from strict adherence to recrimination as modern family values infiltrated the courts. In 1952, the year the Court

---

[89] Armstrong, *California Family Law,* 123.

[90] See e.g., *San Francisco Examiner,* November 27, 1952; *San Francisco Chronicle,* November 26, 1952; and *Sacramento Bee,* November 26, 1952.

[91] *San Francisco Examiner,* November 27, 1952; See also *San Francisco Chronicle,* November 26, 1952.

[92] See e.g., Walter Wadington, "Divorce without Fault," *University of Virginia Law Review* 52:32, 41 (1966); Homer Clark, "Estoppel Against Jurisdictional Attack on Decrees of Divorce," *Yale Law Journal* 70:45, 55 (1960).

[93] George Basye, "Retreat from Recrimination," *California Law Review* 41:320, 320–21 (1953).

decided *DeBurgh,* 32 states adhered to some form of the recrimination doctrine.[94] Many of those states had recently weakened the doctrine by making it discretionary, by adding grounds for divorce, such as "incompatibility," or instituting a policy of "comparative rectitude."[95] *DeBurgh* was not an isolated departure from traditional recrimination doctrine.[96]

Several state courts outside of California used *DeBurgh* to support divorce reform. From 1952 to the so-called "divorce revolution" of 1970—when no-fault divorce began sweeping the country—eight states outside of California cited *DeBurgh* a total of 10 times. Generally those state courts used *DeBurgh* to support public policy-based arguments for divorce reform. After 1970, state courts cited *DeBurgh* nine more times in support of public policy-based arguments against recrimination.

Although *DeBurgh* contributed to the erosion of the recrimination doctrine in various states, its primary significance was that it articulated a policy-based justification for divorce reform, which supported a no-fault divorce scheme. In no-fault divorce proceedings spouses could obtain a divorce without proving that either of them was at fault for the marital breakdown. California adopted the first no-fault divorce statute in 1969 after the Governor's Commission on the Family recommended it along with several other family law reforms. Almost all of the other states followed California by adopting some form of no-fault divorce law as the so-called "divorce revolution" swept the country during the early 1970s.

One of the earliest and most important advocates for no-fault divorce was one-time Traynor clerk and Barbara Armstrong protégée Herma Hill Kay. After clerking for Traynor in 1960, Kay was appointed to fill Armstrong's place on the Boalt faculty. Kay became a leading expert on family law and testified in favor of no-fault divorce at the 1964 California State Assembly Interim Committee on the Judiciary hearings on family law reform.[97] Governor Edmund (Pat) Brown appointed her to the Governor's Commission on the Family in 1966. The commission's report and its proposed Family Court Act, which Kay drafted, created the impetus for California's no-fault divorce statute.

The commission's report and the Family Court Act both drew on Traynor's opinion in *DeBurgh.*[98] They adopted the standard for divorce articulated in *De-*

---

[94]DeBurgh, 39 Cal.2d at 882 citing 2 Vernier, American Family Laws, 87.

[95]Basye, "Retreat from Recrimination," 320, 321.

[96]*Ibid.,* 320; Comment, "California Recrimination Rule Reappraised," *Stanford Law Review* 5:540 (1953).

[97]Herbert Jacob, *Silent Revolution: The Transformation of Divorce Law in the United States* (Chicago, 1988), 52–53.

[98]Kay, "A Family Court," 1205, 1216.

Burgh, at times using Traynor's exact language. *DeBurgh,* the commission, and the Family Court Act each stated that courts should grant divorce when "the legitimate objects of matrimony have been destroyed" and there is "no reasonable likelihood that the marriage can be saved."[99] *DeBurgh* and the commission made the same critique of fault-based divorce. The logical structure and underlying premises of *DeBurgh* and the commission's report also bore a strong resemblance. Even the specific arguments made by Traynor and the commission were strikingly similar. Both, for instance, attacked the concept of marriage as a contract. Both pointed out that the statutory provision making incurable insanity grounds for divorce contravened the notion that divorce required some moral failure constituting fault on the part of a spouse. The commission often used the same language as *DeBurgh*. It viewed divorce as merely symptomatic of "marital breakdown."[100] It articulated a "public interest" in the family "as the basic unit of our society."[101] The law's emphasis on "technical fault"[102] was an "abdication of the public interest in, and responsibility toward, the family"[103] and a "corrupting influence" on marriage.[104]

The adoption of a "breakdown of marriage" standard for divorce was essential to a scheme that emphasized reconciliation rather than fault. Neither Traynor nor the commission advocated divorce by spousal consent.[105] The commission's report specifically addressed the charge that no-fault divorce meant at-will marriage. "We cannot overemphasize," it stated, "that this standard does not permit divorce by consent, wherein marriage is treated as wholly a private contract terminable at the pleasure of the parties without any effective intervention by society." The commission shared Traynor's view of the public interest in marriage. "The intent of this Act is to strengthen marriage," the commission wrote of the Family Court Act.[106] Like Traynor, the commission did not seek to promote individual freedom to the detriment of family life.

---

[99] DeBurgh, 39 Cal.2d at 872; Report of the Governor's Commission on the Family, (December 15, 1966), 31; Family Court Act, Section 028 (reproduced in the Report of the Governor's Commission on the Family, 91).

[100] Report of the Governor's Commission on the Family, 26.

[101] *Ibid.,* 7; DeBurgh, 39 Cal.2d at 863.

[102] Report of the Governor's Commission on the Family, 1; DeBurgh, 39 Cal.2d at 872.

[103] Report of the Governor's Commission on the Family, 7; As noted above Traynor used the phrase "public interest" throughout his opinion.

[104] DeBurgh, 39 Cal.2d at 869. The commission's report refers to "the dissimulation, hypocrisy—and even outright perjury—which is engendered by the present system." Report of the Governor's Commission on the Family, 28–29.

[105] Report of the Governor's Commission on the Family, 23.

[106] *Ibid.,* 60.

Again like Traynor, the commission claimed that the public interest in the family created a judicial responsibility to support the family:

> The standard we propose requires the community to assert its interest in the status of the family, and permits dissolution of the marriage only after it has been subjected to a penetrating scrutiny and the judicial process has provided the parties with all of the resources of social science in aid of conciliation.[107]

The commission proposed the substitution of the existing scheme of family law with a new scheme based on a therapeutic model. Although *DeBurgh* did not propose a therapeutic model for divorce proceedings, Traynor, in the final pages of *DeBurgh,* did describe a role for the divorce court judge that entailed exploration of the "prospects for reconciliation."[108] *DeBurgh* did not explicitly envision divorce court judges who would use counseling services to repair failing marriages. Like the commission, Traynor showed confidence in the capacity of judges to constructively explore the possibility of spousal reconciliation.

Although the Family Court Act embodied fundamental reforms of family law, the commission presented it as a package of technical revisions designed to address the "performance gap" between divorce law *de jure* and divorce law *de facto.*[109] When the commission released its findings in December 1966, they generated no public reaction.[110] The most controversial of the commission's recommendations was not no-fault divorce itself, but the creation of a new Family Court, based on a therapeutic model. Judges resisted this proposal, and the legislature dropped it from its bill.[111] The Democratic legislature passed and Governor Ronald Reagan signed divorce reform legislation with little fanfare in 1969, and the law became effective in 1970.

DeBurgh had an indirect influence on the no-fault movement in that numerous states soon followed California's initiative by adopting their own no-fault statutes. The National Conference of Commissioners on Uniform State Laws (NCCUSL), which promulgated uniform state laws to guide state legislatures, gave further impetus to the "divorce revolution" by proposing its own no-fault divorce statute in 1970. As with the California governor's commission, Herma Hill Kay played a key role in crafting the NCCUSL's model legislation.[112] Like the California statute, the NCCUSL's Uniform Marriage and Divorce Act was packaged as a means of eliminating the gap between the law and the practice of

---

[107]*Ibid.,* 23.

[108]DeBurgh, 39 Cal.2d at 872–73.

[109]Jacob, *Silent Revolution,* 60–61.

[110]*Ibid.,* 56.

[111]*Ibid.,* 58.

[112]*Ibid.,* 71–79.

divorce. The Uniform Marriage and Divorce Act further legitimized no-fault divorce. Immediately after the California legislation and the Uniform Marriage and Divorce Act, no-fault divorce swept the country. By 1975 all but five states had adopted no-fault divorce laws.[113] The lineage of these statutes leads back to Traynor's language in *DeBurgh*. Traynor was the first judge to advance fundamental divorce reform as a remedy for the "performance gap." Not only did he explain the policy justification for no-fault divorce; he helped originate a strategy for effecting divorce reform without controversy.

Conclusion

The story of *DeBurgh* and its influence illustrates the complexity of the relationship between judge-made law and societal attitudes. Attitudes toward divorce, the family, and the role of women were changing in Traynor's day, but societal misgivings about divorce remained widespread. The legislature's aversion to divorce reform before 1970 reflected significant political opposition to easy divorce.[114] However, the ease with which judges granted divorces suggested that societal resistance to easy divorce did little to impede the courts. So did the muted reaction to *DeBurgh,* a decision that significantly changed the framework of California divorce law.

The willingness of trial judges to be lenient in applying the divorce statutes—and the willingness of appellate judges, particularly Traynor, to reform them—meant that divorce law could meet the demands of litigants. The constant flow of divorce cases into the courts worked like a massive litigation campaign, impressing on the courts the desires of the litigants before them. The lower courts did not openly express disagreement with the fault principle, but the operation of divorce law as "law in action" reflected its gradual erosion. Traynor's opinion in *DeBurgh* recognized that the status of women and the institution of marriage had changed, and it responded to the erosion of the fault principle caused by the responsiveness of the lower courts to litigants. Thus, *DeBurgh* reflected not only Traynor's antipathy toward gender inequality in the law, but his assent to the demands of litigants for greater individual freedom within the institution of marriage.

Reforms in divorce law did nothing to quell the tension between the public interest in the family and the interests of individual litigants in divorce. To the contrary, controversy surrounding no-fault divorce increased along with the rising divorce rate during the 1970s. Ultimately judicial efforts to protect the pub-

---

[113]Mintz and Kellogg, *Domestic Revolutions,* 229.

[114]See e.g., Basye, "Retreat from Recrimination," 320, 331.

lic interest in the family gave way to the demands of litigants for divorce. Traynor's conception of the public interest in the family contained the seed of this change. He believed fault-based divorce damaged the institution of marriage, but as events would prove, the elimination of fault removed the most significant obstacle on the road to divorce at-will. Although Traynor did not intend to promote individual freedom to the detriment of family life, no-fault divorce had that effect.

CHAPTER FOUR

People v. Cahan: Police Searches and Cold War Politics

Rarely do judges overrule their own decisions. Not only does the principle of *stare decisis* discourage it, but judges seldom find any reason to reverse themselves. Roger Traynor's opinion in *People v. Cahan,* the first state Supreme Court case to exclude all evidence seized illegally by police, was unusual both because it marked a departure from precedent and because Traynor himself authored the precedent it overruled.[1]

Cahan was a difficult case for Traynor. Years after *Cahan* he reflected on the decision:

> Of all the two-faced problems in the law, there is none more tormenting than the admissibility of illegally obtained evidence. Whichever face one turns to the wall remains a haunting one because there is always that haunting fear that the court has impinged too far on one or the other of the two great interests involved: first, effective law enforcement, without which there can be no liberty; and second, security of one's privacy against arbitrary intrusion by the police.[2]

In *People v. Gonzales,* 13 years before *Cahan,* Traynor rejected arguments for the exclusionary rule and upheld a conviction based on illegally obtained

---

[1]People v. Cahan, 44 Cal.2d 434 (1955).

[2]Roger Traynor, "*Mapp v. Ohio* Still at Large in the Fifty States" (transcription of speech by Traynor at Appellate Judge's Conference, New York, 1964; copy in Traynor Papers, Hastings College of Law).

evidence.[3] Looking back on *Gonzales,* Traynor later wrote, "In 1942 clear academic postulates were as yet unclouded by long judicial experience."[4] Traynor's subsequent experience observing police practices suggested that only the exclusionary rule would deter illegal police searches.

By 1955, the year he decided *Cahan,* Traynor had become worried that the California Supreme Court was acting as an accessory to illegal police practices. He felt the Court had acquired an institutional interest in deterring illegal police searches. "By the time *People against Cahan* came to the court," Traynor wrote, "it had been demonstrated that illegal search and seizure was an ordinary police routine, and that the courts were part of this dirty business because it was owing to our approval that the police were making these illegal searches and seizures."[5] On the basis of what he had learned on the Court, Traynor concluded that only an exclusionary rule would act as a practical deterrent of illegal police searches. "Experience has demonstrated," he wrote, "that neither administrative, criminal nor civil remedies are effective in suppressing lawless searches and seizures."[6]

Cahan raised competing concerns about organized crime and invasive police practices. Prosecutors and police filed *amicus curiae* (friend of the court) briefs arguing that increasingly sophisticated criminal activity demanded increasingly aggressive policing. The American Civil Liberties Union and various civil libertarian defense attorneys filed briefs that expressed their fear of a "police state." The language of Traynor's decision revealed the prevalence of his concerns about police misconduct. Like the civil libertarians, Traynor saw behind the issues raised by *Cahan* the specter of an authoritarian state and a basic threat to civil liberties. A defendant, Traynor wrote in *Cahan,*

> may not be convicted on the basis of evidence obtained by the use of the rack or the screw or other brutal means no matter how reliable the evidence obtained may be. [Citations omitted]. Today one of the foremost public concerns is the police state, and recent history has demonstrated all too clearly how short the step is from lawless although efficient enforcement of the law to the stamping out of human rights.[7]

Traynor felt strongly about illegal police searches. "Few police measures have come to our attention that more flagrantly, deliberately and persistently violated the fundamental principle declared by the Fourth Amendment," his

---

[3]People v. Gonzales, 20 Cal.2d 165 (1942).

[4]Roger Traynor, "*Mapp v. Ohio* at Large in the Fifty States," (1962) *Duke Law Journal* 319, 320.

[5]Traynor, "*Mapp v. Ohio* Still at Large in the Fifty States."

[6]Cahan, 44 Cal.2d at 447.

[7]*Ibid.*

opinion in *Cahan* quoted from an earlier California search-and-seizure case.[8] The threat of communism at home and abroad and the wartime experience with authoritarian regimes raised charged issues that pervaded the ideological environment of the search cases. The presence of civil libertarian themes in *Cahan* reflected the influence of this ideological environment. Traynor's framing of the issues in *Cahan* revealed his apprehension of a "police state," his sympathy with the arguments of the civil libertarians and a historical perspective into which these sentiments fit.

The Factual Context from a Law Enforcement Perspective

Charles Cahan was a bookmaker, convicted on the basis of statements he made in conversations recorded by the police. Los Angeles Police Chief William Parker claimed that Cahan "had most of the illegal horse betters in Los Angeles County as his customers."[9] In an *amicus curiae* brief to the California Supreme Court, Parker described Cahan's organization as extremely sophisticated, involving secret stations where operators would take information from bettors who called in. The operators did not know the names of the people running the operation or even their phone numbers. Cahan's lieutenants would regularly call the secret stations and, using code names, obtain bettor information. The operators at the secret stations kept few if any records—often they recorded bets with chalk or a grease pencil so that the records could be destroyed on a moment's notice. Police Chief Parker estimated the annual take of Cahan's organization at several million dollars.

Parker and the prosecution tried to portray Cahan's case as a contest between law enforcement and organized crime. "[G]ambling in general and bookmaking in particular is one of the greatest sources of money for organized criminal activities," Parker told the court.[10] Parker briefly described 17 murders associated with gambling and organized crime, declaring that Cahan and his henchmen had beaten numerous welshing bettors in an effort to collect debts and had used "strong arm" tactics to compel small-scale bookmakers to join the Cahan organization.[11] Parker further pointed out that while the California Supreme

---

[8]*Ibid.,* quoting Irvine v. California, 347 U.S. 128, 132.

[9]Cahan Court File, Petition to Appear as *Amici Curiae* and to File Briefs in Support of Respondent's Petitions for Hearing and Upon the Merits, and Briefs of *Amici Curiae* in Support of Respondent's Petitions for Hearing, May 13, 1955, Appendix D, Declaration of William Parker. The description of the investigation of Cahan that follows comes largely from this declaration.

[10]*Ibid.*

[11]*Ibid.*

Court was reviewing this case, Cahan awaited trial on charges of strong-arm robbery in a separate case involving the collection of $1,500 from a bettor.

The investigation of Cahan's operation took thousands of hours of police time and involved sophisticated investigative techniques. A thousand hours of surveillance of Cahan yielded little information because Cahan had carefully insulated himself from his operation. The police obtained information through postal inspectors that a Cahan associate named George Tavers regularly received a certain kind of betting form printed only in San Francisco. Based on this information, the police watched Tavers and observed a man named Martin Carr visiting Tavers every day for a few minutes at 9:00 a.m. Every morning Carr took a package from Tavers's house to a house on South Orchard Avenue in Los Angeles, which had been rented by Cahan's brother under an assumed name. Cahan himself never went to the South Orchard address.

In 1950 the Los Angeles Police Department had adopted a written policy for the use of listening devices. In keeping with Los Angeles Police internal policy, the installation of a listening device in the South Orchard house required written permission from Chief Parker, which he gave. A police officer entered the South Orchard house through a window when the house was unoccupied. He did not have a warrant. He installed a listening device in a room that appeared to be an office. The police then spent approximately 1,440 hours listening to and recording the conversations that took place in that room.

When the horse races were over each day, the clerks at the South Orchard house would receive a phone call from a person who turned out to be the organization's bookkeeper. After hundreds of hours of surveillance, police observed one of the clerks meeting with the bookkeeper. The police then followed the bookkeeper to his home on Glenville Drive. The bookkeeper leased the house and lived there with his wife and his six-year-old child. Cahan, his brother, and the bookkeeper frequently met there. With the permission of the owner of the house, the police entered under the guise of termite inspectors and installed a second listening device. Again, they did not have a warrant to enter the house.

The recordings from the Orchard and the Glenville houses were the main evidence against Cahan. Cahan waived jury trial and tried his case in front of a judge, who convicted him and sentenced him to 90 days in the county jail and a $2,000 fine. Despite the light sentence, Cahan appealed.

The prosecution's arguments on appeal attempted to tap the growing fear of crime—particularly fear of organized crime. One current of contemporary political thought coupled crime with the fear of communism. Police Chief Parker became a prominent spokesman for this view. In a speech before the San Diego Barrister's Club and Bar Association in 1952, he asserted that "the three major threats to our freedom were (1) Russian arms; (2) fifth column activities; and (3) crime in this country."[12] Parker's rhetoric drew a parallel between law enforcement and American foreign policy toward the Soviet Union. He described police work "as a containment action with no hope of curing the problem."[13] Just as the fight against communism required a strong, well-equipped military, the fight against crime required "a trained, politics-free professional police force with a national organization to combat organized crime, and freedom to use wire tapping, dictographs and other methods of collecting evidence that are presently in disrepute."[14]

Parker argued that crime was a major cause of "economic loss, political destruction and a symptom of general moral decay."[15] He estimated the population of "professional criminals depending on crime for their living in the U.S. at 6,000,000" and emphasized the sophisticated "machinery of organized crime, particularly the Mafia."[16] Government statistics on crime gave credence to some of Parker's alarmist rhetoric. Federal Bureau of Investigations crime statistics showed a nationwide increase in crime beginning in the 1940s,[17] and the California Department of Justice substantiated this trend. Crime increased rapidly in California in the 1950s and early sixties. During the period 1952 to 1962, the number of reported felonies increased 110 percent from 137,878 to 289,393.[18] California's population increased only 50 percent during the same 10-year period.[19]

The police, prosecutors, and courts tried but failed to keep pace with rising crime. During the period 1952 to 1962, felony arrests increased 70 percent from 58,211 to 98,813.[20] The number of felony arrests per 100,000 rose from 507 in 1952 to 578 in 1962.[21] Arrests more than matched California's population growth, but lagged behind the 110 percent increase in reported felonies. During the period from 1952 to 1962, felony charges in Superior Court increased 240 percent, from 12,926 to 43,851,[22] but felony convictions increased by only 150 percent from 10,923 to 27,084 during the same period.[23] Although, once ar-

---

[12]*Dicta: Newsletter for the Attorneys of San Diego County,* Vol. II, No. 5 (May 1953) 4.

[13]*Ibid.*

[14]*Ibid.*

[15]*Ibid.*

[16]*Ibid.*

[17]Fred Graham, *The Self Inflicted Wound* (New York, 1970), 73.

[18]*Crime in California* (1952), 8; and *Crime in California* (1962), 25.

[19]The population of California was 11,236,900 in 1952. *California Roster* (1952), 230. The population grew to 17,094,000 in 1962. *California Roster* (1962), 158.

[20]*Crime in California* (1952), 12; and *Crime in California* (1962), 47.

[21]*Ibid.*

[22]*Crime in California* (1952), 38; and *Crime in California* (1962), 81.

[23]*Crime in California* (1952), 40; and *Crime in California* (1962), 116.

rested, a suspect was increasingly likely to be charged, the conviction rate decreased significantly. Their failure to stem the rising crime rate created the sense among law enforcement officers that they were losing the war against crime.

Increases in crime contributed to the transformation of the criminal justice system. In their book *The Roots of Justice,* a historical study of the criminal justice system in Alameda County, California, Lawrence Friedman and Robert Percival advance the theory that law enforcement began changing from an adjudicative to an administrative system in the late nineteenth and early twentieth centuries, and that this transformation accelerated during the twentieth century.[24] Among other changes, a professional police force, trained in scientific police techniques, such as finger printing, blood testing, and the use of electronic surveillance equipment, replaced untrained patrolmen. The articles contained in the 1953–1955 issues of *The Journal of Criminal Law, Criminology and Police Science* illustrate the change. The titles include: "The Spectographic Determination of Alcohol in Body Fluids," "The Role of the Pathologic in Arson Investigations," "Utilizing the Lie Detector Technique to Determine the Truth in Disputed Paternity Cases," and "Paper Electrophoresis in the Identification of Writing Inks."[25] Professional prosecutors replaced lawyers appointed by the court to try criminal cases. The focal point of law enforcement shifted from the courts and jury rooms to the streets, station houses, and district attorneys' offices.[26] These changes responded to the demands of an increasingly urban, industrial, crime-threatened state. For police and prosecutors, the increase in crime, and particularly sophisticated organized crime, demanded more professional and more technologically advanced law enforcement. This increasingly administrative character of the law enforcement system created new tensions.[27]

---

[24]Lawrence Friedman and Robert Percival, *The Roots of Justice: Crime and Punishment in Alameda County, California 1870–1910* (Chapel Hill, North Carolina, 1981), 193–94.

[25]Donald Adams, "The Spectographic Determination of Alcohol in Body Fluids," No. 6, *The Journal of Criminal Law, Criminology and Police Science (JCL)* 621; Lester Adelson, "The Role of the Pathologic in Arson Investigations," No. 6, *JCL* 760; Richard Arthur and John Reid, "Utilizing the Lie Detector Technique to Determine the Truth in Disputed Paternity Cases," No. 2, *JCL* 213; "Horizontal Paper Chromatography in the Identification of Ball Point Pen Inks"; Charlotte Brown and Paul Kirk, "Paper Electrophoresis in the Identification of Writing Inks," No. 4, *JCL* 473.

[26]Friedman and Percival, *The Roots of Justice,* 193–94.

[27]James Q. Wilson has argued that concern regarding police discretion to question people on the street, conduct searches and arrest suspects without a warrant generated an effort during the sixties "to bureaucratize, or 'judicialize,' the police: make them subject to more and more explicit rules, have these rules reviewed by the courts or by other non-police agencies, and reduce their discretion wherever possible. . . . The general drift in police management has been to convert, wherever possible, matters of order maintenance

The Factual Context from a Civil Libertarian Perspective

Civil libertarians were concerned about the professionalization of law enforcement and criticized the invasiveness of new law enforcement technology. Morris Grupp, who represented Alfred Berger in *Cahan*'s companion case, compared the prosecution's use of illegally obtained evidence to Senator Joseph McCarthy's attempts to obtain information about government officials whom he suspected of communist sympathies.[28] Grupp and like-minded civil libertarians saw a connection between *Cahan* and anticommunist hysteria. They regarded *Cahan* as a contest between the ideological forces of a police state and the forces attempting to preserve political liberty.

The involvement of the American Civil Liberties Union in criminal cases beginning in the 1950s demonstrated that civil libertarians had come to see those cases as part of their agenda. The ACLU emerged during the World War I era as an organization dedicated to promoting free speech and other constitutional rights.[29] In 1950, ACLU membership was a scant 10,000 and its budget was $100,000.[30] However, beginning that year, ACLU membership doubled every five years and local chapters sprouted around the country.[31] As the ACLU grew into the preeminent civil libertarian organization in the fifties, it expanded its agenda to include the rights of the accused. The ACLU adopted a strategy of filing *amicus* briefs in a few carefully selected criminal cases that raised significant search and seizure issues. In each case they took, ACLU attorneys asked the court to create or extend the exclusionary rule.

The ACLU gradually became involved with search cases during the 1950s, but only after the U.S. Supreme Court had already begun its move toward reform. In the 1949 case of *Wolf v. Colorado,* the U.S. Supreme Court held that the Fourth Amendment applied to the states.[32] The Court did not, however, require the states to adopt the exclusionary rule. The ACLU's efforts to stop illegal police searches began with an appeal to the U.S. Supreme Court three years

---

into matters law enforcement, to substitute the legalistic for the watchman style, and to multiply the rules under which the patrolman operates." James Q. Wilson, *Varieties of Police Behavior: The Management of Law and Order in Eight Communities* (Cambridge, Massachusetts, 1969), 281.

[28]Cahan Court File, Appellant Berger's Reply Brief.

[29]Karen O'Connor and Lee Epstein, *Public Interest Law Groups, Institutional Profiles* (New York, 1989), xiii; Harry N. Scheiber, *The Wilson Administration and Civil Liberties, 1917–1921* (Ithaca, N.Y., 1960).

[30]Robert Rabin, "Lawyers for Social Change: Perspectives on Public Interest Law," *Stanford Law Review* 28: 207, 212 (1970).

[31]*Ibid.*

[32]Wolf v. Colorado, 338 U.S. 25 (1949).

later in *Rochin v. California.*[33] *Rochin* was a major victory for the ACLU. Although the Court refused to impose an exclusionary rule on the states, it held
that the evidence seized by the police in the illegal search of Mr. Rochin violated his fundamental due process rights and had to be excluded at trial.

Despite its victory in *Rochin,* the ACLU did not become involved in other
California search cases during the early fifties. Although *Irvine v. California,* the
next significant U.S. Supreme Court search and seizure case after *Rochin,* presented that opportunity in 1953, the ACLU did not file an *amicus* brief in the
case.[34] In its 1955 petition to submit an *amicus* brief in *Cahan,* the ACLU
claimed to have "repeatedly gone into court to champion fundamental human
rights when these have been threatened, curbed or denied."[35] However, the
ACLU had filed *amicus* briefs in only two California criminal cases prior to
Cahan.[36] Neither of those cases involved search and seizure. Moreover, the
ACLU apparently had nothing to do with *Rochin* as the case made its way
through the state courts.[37] The ACLU became more active after *Cahan.* Its
Southern California Branch filed *amicus* briefs with the California Supreme
Court in eight search and seizure cases after that decision. *Cahan* marked the
beginning of the ACLU litigation campaign for the reform of California's search
and seizure rules.

The attorney most responsible for this litigation strategy was A. L. Wirin,
the chief counsel for the Los Angeles Branch of the ACLU. By 1955, the year
the California Supreme Court decided *Cahan,* Wirin had already gained prominence as a proponent of civil liberties and left-wing causes.[38] He was the first
full-time counsel for the ACLU. Later, as counsel for the National Labor Relations Board, he drew fire for his efforts to assist farm workers. During World
War II, he played an active role in opposing martial law in Hawaii and the in-
ternment of Japanese Americans. Wirin also gained notoriety for representing
accused communists in the Los Angeles and Hawaii Smith Act prosecutions in
the early 1950s.

The climate was hostile to lawyers who represented communists. In 1950
the American Bar Association House of Delegates adopted a resolution calling
for all attorneys to sign a declaration under penalty of perjury regarding their

---

[33]Rochin v. California, 342 U.S. 165 (1952).

[34]Irvine v. California, 347 U.S. 128 (1953).

[35]Cahan Court File, Petition to File *Amicus Curiae* Brief (by the ACLU).

[36]See People v. Stroble, 36 Cal.2d 615 (1951); People v. McCormick, 102
Cal.App.2d Supp. 954 (1951).

[37]People v. Rochin, 101 Cal.App.2d 140 (1950).

[38]Biographical information about Wirin is drawn from his obituary in the *Los Angeles Times,* February 5, 1978, 3, 21.

membership or nonmembership in the Communist Party.[39] In 1951 the ABA House of Delegates voted unanimously to expel communists from the legal profession and called on state bar associations to do the same.[40] The legal community in California heatedly debated proposals aimed at prohibiting communists from becoming lawyers and limiting the ability of lawyers to represent accused communists. In 1955, the California State Bar Board of Governors considered, but ultimately refused to adopt, proposals to disbar attorneys who acted "disrespectfully" toward congressional or legislative committees or who asserted the right against self-incrimination.[41] Lawyers across the state debated these proposals. The *Los Angeles Bar Bulletin* published a forum on the subject, in which prominent members of the bar argued over the Bar proposals.[42] Both sides of the debate claimed to be defending liberty from its ideological foes. Homer Croty, former president of the State Bar, argued, "There is in our opinion no room at the Bar for a Communist. . . . If the subversive lawyer flies the Hammer and Sickle upon his masthead, let him be removed from the State Bar."[43] Opponents of the anticommunist proposals viewed the proposals as a violation of the Fifth Amendment right against self-incrimination, and they associated the threat to their Fifth Amendment rights with the threat of domestic totalitarianism.[44] They abhorred the prospect of being interrogated as suspected criminals. The debate over the anticommunist proposals gave many California attorneys a new appreciation of the rights of the accused. However, in 1955, when the California Supreme Court heard *Cahan,* A. L. Wirin remained a controversial figure. His involvement in *Cahan* and that of the ACLU was a prominent feature of the ideological context of the case.

In 1952, Wirin sued Los Angeles Chief of Police William Parker to enjoin the use of public funds to conduct illegal searches.[45] According to Wirin, illegal police searches were not unusual in Los Angeles or any other part of the state; the police executed the vast majority of searches without warrants. The Los Angeles trial courts, the largest court system in the country, issued only 1,897 war-

---

[39]Michael Belknap, *Cold War Political Justice: The Smith Act, the Communist Party and American Civil Liberties* (Westport, Connecticut), 220.

[40]Belknap, *Cold War Political Justice,* 220.

[41]*The Legal Eagle, A Bulletin for Bench and Bar of the Bay Counties,* Vol. II, No. 13 (April, 1955).

[42]*Los Angeles Bar Bulletin,* "Communism, Professional Freedom and the Conduct of the Bar: A Symposium on Proposed Changes in Rules of Professional Conduct," Vol. 30, No. 6 (March, 1955).

[43]*The Legal Eagle,* Vol. II, No. 13 (April, 1955).

[44]Paul Zifren, "In Opposition to the Proposed Changes in Rules of Professional Conduct," *Los Angeles Bar Bulletin,* Vol. 30, No. 6 (March, 1955).

[45]A. L. Wirin v. William H. Parker, Court File (Hastings Law Library, Volume 8177).

rants from 1930, when the court began keeping track of warrants, to 1968.[46] Before *Cahan* the courts did little to encourage police to obtain warrants. As a result, law enforcement agencies had developed search policies with little judicial oversight or control.

The briefs in *Cahan*—particularly the numerous *amicus* briefs—presented a heated debate over illegal police searches. In response to the Alameda County District Attorney's *amicus* brief, defense attorney Morris Grupp argued to the court, "The ultimate encroachments which lead to a police state are matters of grave public concern, and to declare that the government may commit crimes in order to secure the conviction of a private criminal—would bring terrible retribution."[47] The strong undercurrent of Grupp's argument, echoed in the briefs of other defense attorneys, was the fear of authoritarian government. Contemporary historical awareness gave force to this fear. The phrase "police state" connoted the threat of authoritarianism, like that of Nazi Germany or the Soviet Union under Stalin. For the civil libertarian defense attorneys, McCarthyism portended a "police state" as well. The threat of authoritarianism had a thematic presence throughout their legal briefs. From their perspective, the cause of liberty was very much at stake in the search cases.

Departure from Precedent

What Traynor called the "two-faced" nature of search and seizure law was rooted in the Fourth Amendment of the U.S. Constitution. The Fourth Amendment articulates the principle that unreasonable and unwarranted searches violate fundamental rights. However, it contains ambiguous language regarding the requirements for a legal police search:

> The right of the people to be secure in their persons, houses, papers and effects against unreasonable searches and seizures, shall not be violated, and no Warrants shall issue, but upon probable cause, supported by Oath or affirmation, and particularly describing the place to be searched, and the persons or things to be seized.[48]

The first clause simply prohibits unreasonable searches and seizures, and the second clause creates a warrant requirement for searches, raising the question of when the police must obtain a warrant to execute a search.

---

[46]*Ibid.*

[47]Cahan Court File, Reply Brief of Appellant Alfred Cahan to *Amicus Curiae* Brief of J. F. Coakley, May 23, 1955.

[48]U.S. Constitution, Amendment IV.

The federal judiciary had done little to guide local law enforcement agencies on the requirements of the Fourth Amendment. Until the 1949 case of *Wolf v. Colorado,* the Supreme Court did not require the states to abide by the Fourth Amendment.[49] Even with *Wolf,* the Court did not require the exclusion of evidence illegally obtained by local police.[50] *Wolf* held the states to a somewhat vague standard, based on the Due Process Clause, requiring that law enforcement not violate notions of fundamental fairness in the investigation of suspected criminals. Justice Frankfurter, speaking for the Court, stated that freedom from unreasonable searches and seizures was "implicit in the 'concept of ordered liberty' and as such is enforceable against the States through the Due Process Clause."[51] The Court declined to interfere with states' policies designed to deter illegal searches: "it is not for this Court to condemn as falling below the minimal standards assured by the Due Process Clause a State's reliance upon other methods which, if consistently enforced, would be equally effective."[52] The *Wolf* decision allowed the states to determine the means of enforcing Fourth Amendment rights, and it sent a message to the states that they should consider adopting the exclusionary rule or its equivalent.[53]

Traynor and his brethren heard the Supreme Court's message, but, as Traynor noted, they "clung to the fragile hope that the very brazenness of lawless police methods would bring on effective deterrents other than the exclusionary rule."[54] A succession of illegal search cases made it "abundantly clear that it was one thing to condone an occasional constable's blunder but another thing to condone deliberate and systematic routine invasions of the Fourth Amendment."[55] *Wolf* had created a right without a practical remedy. The cases of *Rochin v. California*[56] and *Irvine v. California*[57] convinced the California Court that it could no longer participate in the "dirty business" of condoning illegal searches.[58]

---

[49]Wolf, 338 U.S. 25.

[50]*Ibid.* The U.S. Supreme Court mandated the exclusionary rule for federal law enforcement officers in 1914. In *Weeks v. United States,* federal law enforcement officials had entered the defendant's house without a warrant and seized papers, which became the basis of a mail fraud prosecution. The Court held that the evidence unfairly prejudiced the trial against the defendant. Weeks v. United States, 232 U.S. 383 (1914).

[51]Wolf, 338 U.S. at 27–28.

[52]*Ibid.,* 31.

[53]See Note, "Two Years with the Cahan Rule," *Stanford Law Review* 9: 515 (1957).

[54]Traynor, "*Mapp v. Ohio* at Large in the Fifty States," 319, 324.

[55]Traynor, "*Mapp v. Ohio* Still at Large in the Fifty States."

[56]Rochin v. California, 342 U.S. 165 (1952).

[57]Irvine v. California, 347 U.S. 128 (1953).

[58]Traynor, "*Mapp v. Ohio* Still at Large in the Fifty States."

The facts of *Rochin* were so disquieting that the U.S. Supreme Court reversed the defendant's conviction on the grounds that the police methods used violated the Due Process Clause of the Fourteenth Amendment. With "some information" that Mr. Rochin had narcotics, the police forced their way into his house, where they found Mr. and Mrs. Rochin in their bedroom.[59] When the police asked about two capsules by the side of the bed, Mr. Rochin put them in his mouth. The police tried to pry the capsules from Mr. Rochin, but ultimately took him to a hospital where a doctor caused the defendant to vomit the capsules by feeding him an emetic solution through a tube. Lab analysis proved that the capsules contained morphine. The California Supreme Court had denied without opinion Rochin's petition for a hearing. However, the case shocked Traynor and some of his colleagues, and they hoped the state attorney general's office would file criminal charges against the police officers responsible for the search.[60] The attorney general took no action.

A year later, in 1953, *Irvine v. California* provided a tougher test of the due process standard for convictions based on illegally obtained evidence. The police had entered Mr. Irvine's home without a warrant three times using a duplicate key, which they had made.[61] They installed a listening device in Mr. Irvine's hall, moved it to his bedroom, and finally moved it again to a bedroom closet. At trial police officers testified to incriminating conversations they heard through the listening devices, and Mr. Irvine was convicted of bookmaking and related offenses. Justice Robert Jackson, writing for the Court, asserted that *Irvine* differed from *Rochin* because it did not involve coercion.[62] The trespass on the defendant's property and the eavesdropping alone provided grounds for a reversal of the conviction.

Justice Jackson expressed doubts about the efficacy of the federal exclusionary rule as a deterrent to illegal searches by federal law enforcement officers.[63] However, his message to the state Supreme Courts was mixed. He argued that "to upset state convictions even before the states have had adequate opportunity to adopt or reject the [exclusionary] rule would be an unwarranted use of federal power."[64] "[S]tate courts may wish to reconsider their evidentiary rules," he suggested.[65] *Irvine* troubled Traynor, and he answered Jackson's ambiguous

---

[59]Rochin, 342 U.S. at 166.

[60]Roger Traynor, "Remarks of Justice Roger J. Traynor at the Conference of Chief Justices in San Francisco, August 1–4 , 1962" (Traynor Papers).

[61]Irvine, 342 U.S. 165.

[62]*Ibid.,* 133.

[63]*Ibid.,* 135.

[64]*Ibid.,* 134.

[65]*Ibid.*

message with a series of decisions that reordered search and seizure rules in California.[66]

Cahan and the search and seizure decisions that followed it demonstrated Traynor's concern over the practical effect of sophisticated police tactics on the privacy rights of individuals. Traynor's rhetoric concerning illegal police searches, though not as heated as the language of the ACLU briefs, revealed a level of indignation with "flagrant violations of the United States Constitution" uncharacteristic of most of his opinions.[67] Traynor feared the prospect of domestic authoritarianism. "Today one of the foremost public concerns is the police state," he wrote, "and recent history has demonstrated all too clearly how short the step is from lawless although efficient enforcement of the law to the stamping out of human rights,"[68] comparable to the abuses of authoritarian regimes abroad.[69] According to long-time California Supreme Court clerk and Traynor confidant Don Barrett, "Traynor was very disturbed by McCarthyism."[70] Barrett, who carpooled with Traynor from Oakland to San Francisco every day, said that Traynor was angered by Boalt Hall professors who refused to speak out against McCarthy. In State Bar disciplinary actions, which could be appealed directly to the California Supreme Court, Traynor opposed punishment of lawyers who refused to deny membership in the Communist Party. His abhorrence of the excesses of anticommunism helped explain his conceptualization of the issues in *Cahan* as an opposition between the police state and civil liberties.

Three of Traynor's seven brethren dissented in *Cahan* while agreeing with him on the illegality of the search.[71] The dissenters pointed first to the "great wealth of legal precedent pointing to the desirability of the continuance of the non-exclusionary rule."[72] Since Traynor's decision did not attempt to hide its departure from precedent, the dissenters could correctly observe:

> [I]f there is any virtue in the doctrine of *stare decisis,* this court should not overturn this firmly established rule in the absence of compelling reasons for such change. The difference in point of view stems from the fact that the majority apparently have found compelling reasons for such change while I have not.[73]

---

[66]Traynor, "*Mapp v. Ohio* Still at Large in the Fifty States."
[67]Cahan, 44 Cal.2d at 436.
[68]Cahan, 44 Cal.2d at 447.
[69]*Ibid.*
[70]Interview with Don Barrett by Ben Field, May 24, 1997.
[71]Cahan, 44 Cal.2d at 453.
[72]*Ibid.*, 452.
[73]*Ibid.*, 453.

While Traynor's opinion expressed concerns about "human rights" and the threat of a "police state," the dissenting justices saw the factual context of *Cahan* from a law enforcement perspective. "[T]he main beneficiaries of the adoption of the exclusionary rule," dissenting Justice Spence wrote, "will be those members of the underworld who prey upon law-abiding citizens through their criminal activities."[74] The dissent did not associate illegal police searches with an authoritarian threat to democratic society. The societal threat on which the dissent focused was "the underworld"—a complex, covert network of criminal activity.

The dissenters and the law enforcement officials who filed briefs in *Cahan* made three main arguments against Traynor's position. Each of these arguments stemmed from their belief that he had overstepped his proper role as a judge. First, the dissenters and law enforcement contended that an exclusionary rule would cause instability in search and seizure law.[75] According to the dissenters,

> If the nonexclusionary rule can be said to have one unquestioned advantage, it is the advantage of certainty. On the other hand, it appears that the exclusionary rule, in the many ramifications of its application to innumerable factual situations, is fraught with such difficulty as to make the formation of satisfactory, certain and workable rules a practical impossibility.[76]

Law enforcement briefs in *Cahan* repeatedly raised concerns that an exclusionary rule would inhibit zealous police work because police officers would not know the legal boundaries that restricted their conduct. The dissenters and law enforcement viewed predictability in search and seizure law as necessary to the maintenance of the rule of law. If the police did not know the rules that governed their conduct because judges changed them, they could not act according to the rules. By making search and seizure law less predictable, Traynor's opinion in *Cahan* would undermine the law and respect for the law.

Second, the dissenters and law enforcement asserted that a judicially created exclusionary rule violated democratic principles. "If . . . of this state," wrote dissenting Justice Spence, "I believe that the Legislature, rather than the courts,

---

[74]*Ibid.*, 457.

[75]The argument for legal stability in criminal procedure became a major theme in the debate over independent state grounds. Opponents of independent state grounds argued that more expansive rights at the state (as opposed to the federal) level would create uncertainty and undermine law enforcement efforts. See Victoria Saker, "Federalism, the Great Writ, and Extrajudicial Politics: The Conference of Chief Justice, 1949–1966," in Harry Scheiber, ed., *Federalism and the Judicial Mind: Essays on American Constitutional Law and Politics* (Berkeley, 1992).

[76]*Ibid.*, 456.

should make such change."[77] The Los Angeles city attorney called the exclusionary rule created by *Cahan* an "intrusion upon the legislative department" and an "experiment in a legislative function."[78] Then-Attorney General Edmund (Pat) Brown and his deputy Arlo Smith argued that because state rules of evidence were legislated, not judicially created, the state Supreme Court could not create an exclusionary rule as a new rule of evidence.[79] Alameda County District Attorney J. F. Coakley made the same argument in his *amicus* brief.[80] The dissenters and law enforcement contended that Traynor went beyond his proper role by making law instead of applying precedent and that he usurped the policymaking authority of the legislature.

Third, opponents of the exclusionary rule argued that the majority in *Cahan* had simply misjudged the need for reform and were making bad policy. The societal problem that demanded attention was organized crime, not illegal police searches. The Los Angeles city attorney, arguing in defense of the Los Angeles Police Department, noted:

> quite a few civil actions are filed against police officers, charging false arrest, false imprisonment, trespass, unlawful search and seizure and the like, but . . . such actions are rarely successful upon trial. Should the Court desire, petitioners can establish that since 1947 there have been approximately 150 civil actions commenced against Los Angeles police officers arising out of their performance of duty. Some of these actions were based upon allegedly unlawful searches. Approximately 200 individual officers have been named as defendants. Nearly $20,000,000 has been claimed as damages, not counting one suit which all by itself asked $60,000,000 in damages. In that time the total recoveries allowed have been less than $5,000 and more than half of that was recovered against six officers in 1948.[81]

According to the Los Angeles city attorney, the number of civil suits against officers demonstrated that people frequently made use of the existing mecha-

---

[77] *Ibid.,* 457.

[78] Cahan Court File, Petition to Appear as *Amici Curiae* and to Briefs in Support of Respondent's Petitions for Hearing and Upon the Merits, and Briefs of *Amici Curiae* in Support of Respondent's Petitions for Hearing, May 13, 1955.

[79] Cahan Court File, Petition for Rehearing, May 11, 1955; Cahan Court File, Supplemental Points and Authorities in Support of Petition for Rehearing (*Berger*), May 28, 1955.

[80] Cahan Court File, *Amicus Curiae* Brief in Support of the Petitions for Rehearing Filed on Behalf of the Plaintiffs and Respondents, May 20, 1955.

[81] Cahan Court File, Petition for Appear as *Amici Curiae* and to File Briefs in Support of Respondent's Petitions for Hearing and Upon the Merits, and Briefs of *Amici Curiae* in Support of Respondent's Petitions for Hearing.

nism for deterring and punishing police misconduct while the almost total failure of plaintiffs to win such civil suits demonstrated that police misconduct was rare.

The Alameda County district attorney said police misconduct was rare, and he emphasized the "menace of the modern criminal syndicate."[82]

[T]echnology, communication and science generally—which some writers are quick to point out have helped the prosecution—have also helped the criminal. In addition, the huge syndicates today have taken advantage of available lawyers and accountants to make not only detection, but prosecution immeasurably more difficult. Crimes of enormous scope are now analytically planned with great detail. Organized crime has enough of an advantage now without being given a greater advantage.[83]

Modern, and more aggressive investigative techniques merely responded to the increasing sophistication of criminal activity.

The dissenters and other critics expressed doubts about the effectiveness of an exclusionary rule as a deterrent. Citing the U.S. Supreme Court in *Irvine* the dissent referred to the federal exclusionary rule as "'no more than a mild deterrent at best.'"[84] The Alameda County district attorney cited to the Court a study concluding that in Michigan, where the legislature had adopted the exclusionary rule, armed robberies had increased dramatically because of the release from custody of people illegally searched and found to be unlawfully carrying concealed weapons.[85] The dissenters and law enforcement asserted not only that Traynor's policy objective was misguided, but that the exclusionary rule—the means toward achieving his objective—would fail.

Cahan and the Coherence of Pragmatic Reform

In the series of search and seizure cases that followed *Cahan,* Traynor sought to craft a practical policy that could withstand the attacks of its critics. This effort brought his opinions into direct conflict with those who opposed judicial activism. Traynor understood that *Cahan* created uncertainty among judges, lawyers, and law enforcement personnel, and so he attempted to formulate "workable

---

[82]Cahan Court File, *Amicus Curiae* Brief in Support of the Petitions for Rehearing Filed on Behalf of the Plaintiffs and Respondents, May 20, 1955.

[83]*Ibid.*

[84]Cahan, 44 Cal.2d at 455.

[85]Cahan Court File, *Amicus Curiae* Brief in Support of the Petitions for Rehearing Filed on Behalf of the Plaintiffs and Respondents.

rules" that reflected a clear policy objective.[86] Judicial changes in criminal procedure are generally recognized as involving instability in the law.[87] Traynor believed, however, that the demand for an effective deterrent to illegal police searches simply outweighed the detriments of legal uncertainty. In response to the criticism that he had usurped the legislature's authority, he contended that the judiciary was better able to reform the common law than was the legislature. In 1956, the year after *Cahan,* he wrote a law review article entitled "Law and Social Change in a Democratic Society" outlining this position.[88] Realizing that *Cahan* had the potential to damage the reputation of the Court, he used a series of subsequent search and seizure opinions to dispel the notion that the Court lacked sensitivity to the threat of organized crime or the legitimate needs of law enforcement.

The main thrust of *Cahan* and its progeny was to provide a policy-based justification for the exclusionary rule. In contrast with the U.S. Supreme Court's later decision in *Mapp v. Ohio,* which deemed the exclusionary rule "an essential part of both the Fourth and the Fourteenth Amendments," Traynor explained his decision in *Cahan* as the means to achieve the policy objective of deterring illegal police searches.[89] The rationale of *Cahan* sent ripples through the body of California search and seizure case law. In the years following *Cahan,* Traynor systematically revised rules of search and seizure, making them into a "reasonably orderly constellation."[90] "If we keep in mind that the *raison d'être* of the exclusionary rule is the deterrence of lawless law enforcement," Traynor wrote, "we can guard against confusion in the attendant rules we develop."[91] The objective of *Cahan* defined in this way influenced every significant search and seizure case that Traynor decided after 1955—whether it dealt with consent to search, the "knock-notice rule," search incident to arrest, or other related issues. Traynor's search and seizure opinions sought intellectual coherence through the consistent pursuit of a policy objective—the deterrence of illegal police searches.

In the two years following *Cahan* the California Supreme Court and lower appellate courts in California decided over 100 search and seizure cases.[92] While *Cahan* made clear his concern about the Fourth Amendment rights of the accused,[93] Traynor noted that "our police . . . have a heroic job to do," and he

---

[86]Cahan, 44 Cal.2d at 451.
[87]Craig Bradley, *The Failure of the Criminal Procedure Revolution* (Philadelphia, 1993).
[88]Traynor, "Law and Social Change in a Democratic Society," 230.
[89]Mapp v. Ohio, 367 U.S. 643, 657 (1961).
[90]Traynor, "*Mapp v. Ohio* at Large in the Fifty States, 319, 323.
[91]*Ibid.*
[92]Note, "Two Years with the Cahan Rule," 515, 536.
[93]Cahan, 44 Cal.2d at 442.

commended police officers for their difficult and dangerous work.[94] His search and seizure opinions often condoned police actions because Traynor's deterrence-based rationale did not always require the exclusion of evidence. For instance, good faith mistakes by the police resulting in illegal searches did not require the exclusion of evidence. Traynor intended only to deter knowing violations of the Fourth Amendment, he did not seek to penalize law enforcement for mistakes that the exclusionary rule could not deter. In *People v. Gorg,* the owner of a home in which Mr. Gorg occupied a room consented to a police search of the room.[95] Traynor ruled that the marijuana found during the search was admissible at trial even though the owner lacked the authority to consent to the search of Gorg's private quarters. The police had acted reasonably and in good faith on the owner's consent. Therefore, the search, though illegal, did not implicate the deterrence rationale of *Cahan.*[96]

Traynor created a similar "good faith" exception to the knock notice rule, which required police to announce their presence before entering a dwelling. The police had seen heroin users come and go from an apartment many times during their month-long surveillance of the apartment. Joined by a cooperative heroin user, they approached the front door, and the heroin user knocked. When the police heard a voice inside yell "wait a minute" and then the sound of retreating feet, they kicked in the door, searched the apartment, and found heroin. Although the officers violated the knock notice rule, Traynor refused to allow the formal requirements of the law to stand in the way of effective law enforcement. The court waived the requirements of the knock notice statute because the officers reasonably believed compliance with the statute would allow a suspected criminal to escape or destroy evidence.[97]

The *Cahan* rationale also influenced the rules of arrest. Traynor worried that once the police had made an arrest and found evidence of a crime, the evidence would be used as a retroactive justification for the arrest.[98] In other words, protections against illegal searches of a person were only as good as the protections against arrest without probable cause. *People v. Brown* prohibited the police from searching illegally arrested suspects without triggering the exclusionary rule.[99] The police watched Ms. Brown walk in front of their car carrying something clenched in her fist. They approached her from behind and grabbed

---

[94]Roger Traynor, "Lawbreakers, Courts, and Law-Abiders," *Missouri Law Review* 31:181, 206 (1966).

[95]People v. Gorg, 45 Cal.2d 776, 780–81 (1955).

[96]*Ibid.*

[97]People v. Maddox, 46 Cal.2d 301, (1956); Also People v. Moore, 140 Cal.App.2d 657, (1956).

[98]Traynor, "*Mapp v. Ohio* at Large in the Fifty States, 319, 333.

[99]People v. Brown, 45 Cal.2d 640 (1955).

her wrists. Then they identified themselves and asked her to open her hand, but she refused. So they forced open her hand and took from her a small rubber container. Lab analysis showed the contents of the container to be heroin. Traynor, writing for the Court, reasoned that the police must have probable cause to arrest before arresting a suspect and conducting a search incident to the arrest. The police lacked probable cause to arrest Ms. Brown, and therefore they lacked a justification for their search. Citing *Cahan,* Traynor argued that to condone the search of Ms. Brown would "destroy the efficacy of the exclusionary rule."[100]

The rationale of *Cahan* protected criminal defendants from searches incident to arrest predicated on illegal arrests. However, it also justified an exception to the exclusionary rule where the police arrested a suspect illegally, but in good faith. In *People v. Chimmel,* police officer DeComa obtained an arrest warrant that turned out to be invalid.[101] DeComa and other officers arrested Chimmel at his home. They thoroughly searched his house and garage and found stolen coins. Despite the invalidity of the arrest warrant, the Court (with Traynor concurring) decided not to invalidate the search incident to arrest.[102] "No evidence even intimates that DeComa procured the [arrest] warrant in bad faith or exploited the illegality of the warrant," Justice Tobriner wrote.[103] The Court held that DeComa's good faith reliance on the magistrates' finding of probable cause saved the arrest and the search. The U.S. Supreme Court ultimately overturned Chimmel's conviction on other grounds;[104] and unlike the California Court, the U.S. Supreme Court would later require the exclusion of illegally obtained evidence, even in cases of good faith.[105] The U.S. Supreme Court made the exclusionary rule a constitutional requirement when the police illegally seized evidence.[106] This principled approach contrasted with Traynor's policy-based rationale and led to different results than the California Court reached.

Traynor recognized the impermanence of judicial decisions, including his own. This notion militated against broad statements of principle and impelled

[100]*Ibid.,* 644.

[101]People v. Chimmel, 68 Cal.2d 436 (1968).

[102]*Ibid.*

[103]*Ibid.,* 444.

[104]The U.S. Supreme Court overturned Chimmel's conviction on the grounds that, even if the arrest was valid, the subsequent warrantless search of Chimmel's house violated the Fourth Amendment. The Court held that a search incident to arrest could not expand beyond the area in the arrestee's immediate control. Chimmel v. California, 395 U.S. 752 (1969).

[105]See e.g., Aguilar v. Texas, 378 U.S. 108 (1964); and Spinelli v. U.S., 393 U.S. 410 (1969).

[106]The U.S. Supreme Court later created an exception to this rule in *U.S. v. Leon,* 468 U.S. 897 (1984).

him to respond to new demands placed on the law. The absence of an effective deterrent to illegal searches created one such demand. Traynor's response, in the series of cases beginning with *Cahan,* may obscure his appreciation of the transitory nature of his own decisions. However, it is significant that his tool for protecting Fourth Amendment rights was a judicial rule of evidence, not a broad statement of principle. He intended his "workable rules" for search and seizure to endure only so long as they remained "workable rules." The ideal judge, he declared, "can write an opinion that gives promise of more than a three-year lease on life by accurately anticipating the near future."[107] Traynor's understanding of the ephemeral nature of the law fostered both activism and humility.

Reactions to *Cahan*

Cahan provoked a strong, negative reaction from some Californians, and Traynor worried about attacks on the Court in response to *Cahan.*[108] He feared the Court might become the scapegoat for rising crime,[109] but signs of public discontent with the Court's positions on criminal procedure appeared only occasionally. The 1958 Los Angeles County Grand Jury took the unusual step of issuing an extensive report condemning *Cahan* and other Court decisions:

> This ridiculous overliberality of interpretation of our constitution reflects a dangerous softness of thinking and a weak and watery philosophy, on the part of these people whom we put into a position to make such important decisions.[110]

The Grand Jury even called for the removal of four justices from office, but no credible campaign against the justices emerged.[111]

The liveliest debate over the Court's actions took place on the pages of California newspapers. Some newspapers attacked the Court as procriminal. The *San Francisco Examiner* reported that *Cahan* was "a change that gave the criminal defendant the greatest break he had ever received."[112] In a six-article series on the Court's search and seizure cases, the *Examiner* claimed that *Cahan* and its progeny were disastrous:

---

[107]Roger Traynor, "No Magic Words Could Do It Justice," *California Law Review* 49:615, 625 (1961).
[108]Roger Traynor, "Givers and Takers of the Law," *Journal of Public Law,* Vol. 18, No. 2, 247, 251 (1969).
[109]*Ibid.* at 253.
[110]*Los Angeles Daily Journal,* December 23, 1958.
[111]*Ibid.*
[112]*San Francisco Examiner,* April 29, 1956.

The initial blast by the four justices was followed by twenty-three aftershocks in the succeeding ten months. Some of these struck the law enforcement officers with even more devastating effect than the granddaddy effusion of April 27, 1955 [*Cahan*]. Before the last one subsided, criminal justice in California had acquired a distinctly new look. The supreme court had rewritten the rule book on the law of arrest and on many phases of criminal procedure—and the revisions were drastic.[113]

The *Examiner* characterized the Court's search and seizure decisions as both damaging to law enforcement and destructive to the Court's reputation. Other newspapers did not share the *Examiner*'s view. The *San Francisco Chronicle* editorial board came out in favor of *Cahan:*

> For half a century the Constitutions of the United States and of the State of California have not meant what they said in protecting "the right of the people to be secure in their persons, houses, papers and effects against unreasonable searches and seizures" by the police in California. They do now.[114]

The *Los Angeles Times* and the *Sacramento Bee* also supported the Court.[115] To the extent that the newspapers made or reflected public opinion, public opinion on the Court's search and seizure decisions diverged depending on whether the source favored law enforcement or civil liberties.

Response of the Legal Community

The majority decision in *Cahan* generated considerable debate within the legal community. The *Journal of the State Bar* published various articles on *Cahan,* some critical, some supportive, including an article by Traynor himself. The Criminal Courts Bar Association, a Los Angeles County organization dominated by defense attorneys, and the Marin County Bar Association each filed an *amicus* brief on the defendant's behalf in *Cahan*.[116] In a vote of Marin Bar Committee members, 19 of 28 members favored a motion to file the *amicus* brief. The seven members opposed to the brief were from the district attorney's office.[117] Perhaps because of the excesses of anticommunism, many lawyers viewed with skepticism the law enforcement position in *Cahan*.

---

[113]*Ibid.*

[114]*San Francisco Chronicle,* April 29, 1955.

[115]See *Los Angeles Times,* May 1, 1955; and *Sacramento Bee,* May 7, 1955.

[116]Cahan Court File, Brief of *Amicus Curiae* (Criminal Briefs Volumes 8173 and 8177, Hastings Law Library).

[117]*Ibid.*

In academic circles *Cahan* gained recognition as an important case, and contributors to the major California law reviews generally cited *Cahan* approvingly.[118] The *California Law Review* and *Stanford Law Review* reported the decision soon after the Court handed it down. The *Hastings Law Journal* and *Southern California Law Review* first cited *Cahan* in articles on *Mapp v. Ohio*. Most national law reviews outside of California published articles citing *Cahan*.[119] However, with the exception of the *Minnesota Law Review*, none of the national law reviews mentioned *Cahan* in the 1950s. Most of them first mentioned *Cahan* in the early 1960s in the context of a discussion of *Mapp*. Lawyers, judges, and law professors outside of California first viewed *Cahan* as an important decision because of its influence on the U.S. Supreme Court.

In the 1960 case of *Elkins v. United States*, the U.S. Supreme Court struck down the so-called "silver platter doctrine," which permitted state law enforcement personnel to provide illegally obtained evidence for use in federal cases despite the prohibition on the use of such evidence gathered by federal law enforcement officers.[120] The Court's opinion referred to the "experience in California" as "most illuminating," noting *Cahan*'s finding that alternatives to the exclusionary rule had proved ineffective.[121] Chief Justice Earl Warren, the author of *Mapp*, singled out the reasoning in *Cahan* for discussion, while merely citing some of the other states' laws adopting an exclusionary rule. More importantly, the Court took *Cahan* as confirmation that other remedies for illegal searches besides the exclusionary rule had failed. *Wolf* had posed the question of whether other remedies could work. *Cahan* answered that other remedies had not worked. *Mapp* relied on *Cahan* as the main precedent for this essential proposition.

Not a single state court outside of California cited *Cahan* before 1961, the year the U.S. Supreme Court decided *Mapp*. When, in 1949, the U.S. Supreme Court decided *Wolf*, compelling the states to meet the requirements of the Fourth Amendment, 19 states had already adopted some form of exclusionary rule.[122] Between *Wolf* and *Mapp* only five states, including California, adopted an ex-

---

[118]By major California law reviews I mean, *California Law Review, Stanford Law Review, Hastings Law Journal*, and *Southern California Law Review*.

[119]By national law reviews outside California, I mean *Columbia Law Review, Chicago Law Review, Georgetown Law Journal, Harvard Law Review, Michigan Law Review, Minnesota Law Review, New York University Law Review, University of Pennsylvania Law Review, Texas Law Review, Virginia Law Review*, and *Yale Law Journal*.

[120]Elkins v. United States, 364 U.S. 206 (1960).

[121]*Ibid.*, 364.

[122]See *ibid.*, 224–231; and "The Supreme Court, 1960 Term," *Harvard Law Review*, 75:152, 154, footnote 398 (1961).

clusionary rule.[123] Of these five states, the only state to significantly change its policy regarding illegal searches after *Cahan* was North Dakota, which made statutory changes in 1960.[124] Most states that adopted an exclusionary rule without a U.S. Supreme Court directive had already done so by the time the California Supreme Court decided *Cahan*. State court judges frequently cited *Cahan,* but only after *Mapp* required them to reorder their search and seizure rules. After 1961, 45 state court opinions outside of California cited *Cahan* (seven of them in dissenting opinions). Appellate judges in other states used *Cahan* primarily to explain the policy rationale behind the search and seizure rules they adopted. It is significant that these judges generally did not embrace Traynor's creative approach toward judging. Instead, they used Traynor's opinions more narrowly as legal precedent.

Was *Cahan* A Self-Inflicted Wound?

Up to that time, *Cahan* was the most controversial decision Traynor had made, and it generated the most vociferous reaction. According to Don Barrett, Traynor received hate mail in response to his decision.[125] Law enforcement vocally opposed the Court's search and seizure decisions. Los Angeles Police Chief Parker blamed *Cahan* for a 35.8 percent increase in the crime rate in Los Angeles during the first quarter of 1956.[126] The Oakland Police Chief claimed the decision "placed a stumbling block in the way of law enforcement officers."[127] James Don Keller, district attorney and county counsel of San Diego County, spoke for the majority of prosecutors and police officers when he wrote:

> At a time when the State of California and practically every area of the State was experiencing a tragic increase in narcotic traffic, the *Cahan* decision was not far short of disastrous to State and local agencies charged with responsibility for enforcement of the narcotics laws. . . . In bookmaking operations, while street bookmakers or collectors may be arrested, the principals in the operation transact their dealings by telephone and make few, if any personal contacts, this surveillance is of no value.[128]

---

[123]*Ibid.*

[124]Mapp, 367 U.S. at 652.

[125]Interview with Don Barrett by Ben Field, May 24, 1997.

[126]*San Francisco Chronicle,* April 6, 1956.

[127]*San Francisco Chronicle,* April 21, 1955.

[128]"Note, "Two Years with the Cahan Rule," 515, 538.

Traynor worried about the perception that "due process rules are the source of all our woes," and he felt the need to defend the Court in his writings.[129] He noted that no empirical study proved a correlation between crime and court rules.[130] "[T]hose who equate due process rules with coddling of criminals have failed dismally," he wrote, "to explain why crime flourishes when there is no such so-called coddling."[131] In 1962 Traynor reported that "there has been a substantial abatement of the fear that the [*Cahan*] rule would frustrate law enforcement. It has become increasingly clear that acceleration of crime in our state, as in others, cannot be explained by the simplistic reference to the presence or absence of the exclusionary rule."[132] With time the new search and seizure rules announced by the California Supreme Court seemed less onerous to law enforcement. Edmund Brown, who opposed *Cahan* when he served as attorney general in 1955, later admitted that it improved the quality of law enforcement. The new rules gained acceptance as police departments gradually incorporated them into their police training programs.

Public fear of crime and the perception that the "liberalization" of criminal procedure fostered crime did not become a force for counter-reform in California, as it did in national politics during the late sixties. In his book *The Self-Inflicted Wound,* Fred Graham argued that the U.S. Supreme Court's "criminal revolution" nearly destroyed the Court's all-important reputation as the conscience of society.[133] By 1968 racial animosity and urban riots had charged the debate over the rights of criminal defendants. Congress included in the Omnibus Crime Control and Safe Streets Act of 1968 a provision designed to reverse *Miranda v. Arizona.*[134] Although the anti-Supreme Court provisions did not go into effect, they signified the strength of the reaction to the Court's criminal procedure reforms.

The atmosphere surrounding the California Supreme Court's criminal procedure decisions and the objectives behind them differed significantly from those of the U.S. Supreme Court. Consciousness of the disparate treatment of racial minorities by the criminal justice system and fear of racial violence did not yet animate controversies over criminal procedure decisions in the 1950s.[135]

---

[129]Traynor, "Lawbreakers, Courts, and Law-Abiders," 181, 187.

[130]*Ibid.,* 204.

[131]*Ibid.*

[132]Traynor, "*Mapp v. Ohio* at Large in the Fifty States," 319, 323.

[133]Graham, *The Self-Inflicted Wound,* 5.

[134]*Ibid.,* 12, 121.

[135]This is not to say, by any means, that racism and disparate treatment were absent from California's law enforcement or criminal justice. For analysis of several incidents that did gain prominence in public debate, see Ricardo Romo, "Southern California and the Origins of Latino Civil Rights Activism," *Western Legal History* 3:379–406 (1990).

Although the California Court's "liberalizing" decisions had some vocal critics, pressure external to the judiciary had little effect on the reform of criminal procedure in California. *Cahan* and its progeny were not a "self-inflicted wound" to the California Supreme Court's reputation. Unlike the Court's rulings on death penalty cases during the 1970s, they caused no significant immediate political damage to the Court. To the contrary, they contributed to the Court's reputation for leadership within the legal community.

Conclusion

Cahan and its progeny exemplified Traynor's conception of judicial creativity. Like the Pragmatist philosophers, Traynor believed that judgment was the process of bringing experience to bear on the facts. His experience on the bench impelled him to overrule his own decision, *Gonzales,* when he realized it had failed to deter illegal searches, and he crafted new rules to serve that function. *Cahan* and its progeny functioned as a coherent system of rules instituted because of the need for a practical, policy-oriented approach to the problem of illegal police searches. Traynor called on judges to assert judicial control over law enforcement procedures. He believed the health of the law required that law enforcement yield to judicial authority. He stood for the belief that the prestige and the institutional self-interest of the Court also depended on this assertion of authority.

Though it was controversial, Traynor's analysis had significant persuasive force. As the states wrestled with the problem of illegal police searches, U.S. Supreme Court cases, culminating in *Mapp,* pushed them toward the adoption of an exclusionary rule. Finally, Traynor gave clear policy reasons, based on observation of police practices, for the departure from precedent. His innovations in search and seizure law reflected his civil libertarian sympathies, and the reaction of the legal community also reflected increased concern about the protection of civil liberties. *Cahan* and its progeny incorporated into law these changing value judgments on police tactics.

Ben Field

Justices from left to right: Marshall F. McComb; Louis H. Burke; Mathew O. Tobriner; Roger J. Traynor, chief justice; Stanley Mosk; Raymond L. Sullivan; and Raymond E. Peters (1966). Photo courtesy of the California Supreme Court.

CHAPTER FIVE

The Product Liability Cases: Judicial Activism and Consumerism

Roger Traynor's tenure on the bench coincided with the emergence of mass marketing and mass consumption as dominant features of middle-class economic life. As the middle class expanded after World War II, new amenities became more available and mass marketing reached new levels. Increasingly, Americans sought a sense of self-fulfillment and material security in product consumption. Purchasing power was liberating; it meant the freedom to buy and the ability to obtain new labor-saving products. However, with this newfound freedom came new risks. Consumers based their spending choices on information gleaned primarily from advertising and marketing. They had little familiarity with the sources of the products they bought and only limited recourse against faraway manufacturers if dissatisfied with their purchases.

The rise of mass marketing and mass consumption after World War II shaped Traynor's views on the law of producer/consumer relations. He believed consumers' legal rights against producers had not kept pace with economic changes. In his 1944 concurrence in *Escola v. Coca-Cola Bottling Company* Traynor set forth his theory that manufacturers should be held strictly liable for consumer injuries caused by design or manufacturing defects.[1] Nineteen years later all of Traynor's colleagues joined his opinion in *Greenman v. Yuba Power Products, Inc.*, making the California Supreme Court the first court to adopt a rule of strict product liability.[2]

---

[1] Escola v. Coca-Cola Bottling Company, 24 Cal.2d 453 (1944).
[2] Greenman v. Yuba Power Products, Inc., 59 Cal.2d 57 (1963).

The rule that made manufacturers strictly liable for the products they put on the market was the most important doctrinal development in tort law during the late 20th century. Strict liability had far-reaching consequences for businesses. It altered the legal relationships of the marketplace by shifting responsibility for consumer injuries to businesses, and it forced businesses to insure themselves against the risk of consumer injuries. Critics of the doctrine raised concerns about its fairness and its efficacy, but the doctrine became firmly entrenched in American law.

The Cases of *Escola v. Coca-Cola* and *Greenman v. Yuba Power Products, Inc.*

One day in 1942, Gladys Escola, a waitress at Tiny's Waffle Shop in Merced, California, was loading bottles of Coca-Cola into a restaurant refrigerator when one of them exploded in her hand. Glass from the bottle caused a deep five-inch cut across her palm, severing nerves and muscles. She went to a surgeon, who operated on her under general anesthesia, but the accident left her with permanent disability. She could no longer shake hands, carry weight, or comb her hair. Escola made a claim for workman's compensation, but received only $42.60, which did not even cover her medical expenses and lost wages.[3] So she sued several Coca-Cola subsidiaries, including the Coca-Cola Bottling Company of Fresno.

The Coke bottle that injured Escola had been delivered to Tiny's by a truck driver for the Coca-Cola Bottling Company. After delivery the Coke bottles sat in boxes behind the restaurant counter for at least 36 hours. Several witnesses, including Ms. Escola, testified at the trial about the explosion. No one said that Escola or anyone else at the restaurant had mishandled the bottles. Escola's trial attorney, the famous "King of Torts" Melvin Belli, called one of the bottling company's truck drivers as a witness at trial. The truck driver testified that he had seen other Coca-Cola Bottling Company bottles explode spontaneously in the past. Two engineers testified as witnesses for the Coca-Cola Bottling Company. Each suggested that Escola's injuries did not result from Coca-Cola's negligence. Belli vigorously attacked both witnesses on cross-examination. One of them had testified for Coca-Cola in several exploding bottle cases previous to *Escola,* and Belli made him out to be a company apologist. At every opportunity Belli cast his client as the innocent victim of a large, distant, uncaring corporation.

Belli did not try to prove the bottling company had committed a specific act constituting legal negligence. No specific act showed that the bottling company

---

[3]Escola v. Coca Cola Court File, Opening Statement by Melvin Belli, Reporter's Transcript on Appeal, September 17, 1942, California State Archives, Sacramento.

had failed to exercise "due care" in the handling of the particular bottle that injured Gladys Escola. Instead, Belli argued the doctrine of *res ipsa loquitur* (literally translated, the thing speaks for itself). Under that doctrine a defendant could be found liable for an injury if the defendant had exclusive control of the thing that caused the injury and the circumstances of the injury would ordinarily not occur in the absence of the defendant's negligence. The jury agreed with Belli that the bottle that injured Ms. Escola must have been defective when it left the Bottling Company because Coke bottles do not ordinarily explode when handled, and it found the bottling company liable.

On appeal to the California Supreme Court in 1944, lawyers for the bottling company argued that the company should not be held liable for the injury because the bottle in question had left the company's control. Chief Justice Phil Gibson's majority opinion upheld the jury's verdict, stating, "under the more logical view . . . the doctrine (of *res ipsa loquitur*) may be applied upon the theory that defendant had control at the time of the negligent act."[4] Gibson's opinion recognized that many state courts had applied *res ipsa loquitur* to exploding bottle cases and many had not. He found some support in California case law for both positions. He concluded, however, that the underlying reason for the "exclusive control" requirement of the doctrine was to "eliminate the possibility that it was the plaintiff who was responsible."[5]

Traynor agreed with Gibson's result, but he went beyond Gibson's opinion by arguing for the adoption of a new theory of product liability. Traynor's concurrence explained in detail his view that "the manufacturer incurs absolute liability when an article that he has placed on the market . . . proves to have a defect that causes injury to human beings."[6] Even Traynor's majority opinion in *Greenman v. Yuba Power,* which would adopt a strict liability standard in 1963, did not explain his reasoning as thoroughly as his *Escola* concurrence. His *Greenman* opinion simply stated, "we need not recanvass the reasons for imposing strict liability" and cited *Escola* among other cases and law review articles. Traynor's *Escola* concurrence was his most substantial articulation of his argument for strict liability. Belli later referred to Traynor's concurrence as the beginning of a "tort revolution."[7]

In his terse six-page *Greenman* opinion, Traynor and his brethren became the first state Supreme Court to adopt the strict liability standard in a product liability case.[8] William Greenman was a dentist whose hobby was furniture

---

[4]Escola, 24 Cal.2d at 458.

[5]*Ibid.,* 458.

[6]*Ibid.,* 461.

[7]Melvin Belli ed., *Trial and Tort Trends 1964–65 Seminar* (Indianapolis, 1965), 3.

[8]In *Henningsen v. Bloomfield Motors* 161 A.2d 69 (1960) the New Jersey Supreme Court held that a car manufacturer and a car dealer could be liable for injuries caused by a defective steering wheel to a car buyer's wife. The court held there was an implied

making. He received a power tool, called a Shopsmith, as a Christmas gift from his wife in 1955. In 1957 he used the Shopsmith as a lathe to make a wooden chalice. After working on the wood several times with the Shopsmith, the tool malfunctioned, sending the wood flying into Greenman's head, causing serious injury. He began bleeding from his eye, and spinal fluid leaked from his nose. During the surgery that followed a metal plate was inserted into his head. The injury prevented him from doing various physical activities, like leaning over and running. After almost 11 months, Greenman sued Yuba Power Products, which manufactured the Shopsmith, and The Hayseed, the store that sold it to his wife.

At trial, Greenman's lawyers offered two theories of the manufacturer's liability. First, they argued that Yuba Power had violated the terms of its express warranty that the Shopsmith could be used as a lathe without danger. Greenman testified at trial that he read the Yuba Power brochure advertising the Shopsmith as a combination lathe, saw, and drill. His lawyers argued that this brochure created a warranty that the Shopsmith could be used safely as a lathe. Second, they claimed that Yuba Power had been negligent in the design of the Shopsmith. They presented expert testimony that vibrations during the normal use of the tool loosened the mechanism for holding in place the wood being carved by the lathe. This defect allowed the wood to fly out of the lathe. After a trial that lasted several days the jury found Yuba Power liable for $65,000, but decided The Hayseed was not liable at all.

Yuba appealed. The jury verdict did not indicate whether Yuba's liability arose from its warranty or its negligence or both. This "general verdict" required Yuba to argue against both theories of liability on appeal. Yuba's attacks on the negligence theory, however, seemed weak. The testimony of Greenman's experts clearly constituted evidence legally sufficient to support the verdict, and the trial judge had used well-established, standardized jury instructions to explain the law of negligence. Yuba focused its attack on the warranty theory. Since the general verdict would likely withstand appeal even if an appellate court agreed that Yuba was not liable on a warranty theory, the purpose of the appeal appears to have been in part to establish a precedent that would hinder future lawsuits grounded on warranty theory. Manufacturers and insurers did not present an industry response to *Greenman*. One company, the Plastic Process Company, which faced a lawsuit with similar issues, filed an *amicus* brief in support of Yuba, but either Yuba or its insurance company, whichever sponsored the appeal, appears to have recognized the long-term strategic importance of opposing the warranty claim.

---

warranty of merchantability that extended beyond the person who bought the car. Without adopting a strict liability standard the New Jersey Court reached a similar result.

The Rise of Consumerism and Product Liability Litigation

The rise of mass consumption and mass marketing after World War II transformed economic life in California. As the *California Blue Book, 1950* noted:

> The per capita average of retail sales in California during 1948 was . . . 26 percent higher than the United States average. . . . In some categories of trade, such as eating places, furniture and home furnishings, building materials and hardware, and drug stores, the differential was somewhat higher. This is due mostly to higher levels of income and higher average standards of living.[9]

More than most Americans, Californians ate at restaurants, bought furniture and household appliances at department stores, and consumed new cosmetics and hygiene-related products. They bought canned and bottled beverages in great quantities, and all of these consumer industries grew rapidly after World War II.[10]

The Coke bottle was a prototypical product of the consumer economy—it came to symbolize consumerism in Andy Warhol prints—and exploding bottle cases were the prototypical product liability lawsuit. In his brief to the court, Belli commented on the frequency of exploding bottle cases.[11] He described an insurance company advertisement in *Colliers Magazine* in which

> we find the picture of a startled yet happy individual taking a bottle of beverage from an ice chest. He is startled because the bottle is exploding, but he is at the same time happy (at least the advertisement would have us believe) because he knows that a certain insurance company, which inserted the add [*sic*], will pay him $10,000 for the loss of an eye from an exploding bottle! The caption of the both disastrous yet happy event is "Injured by exploding bottle."

Exploding bottle cases found their way into the popular consciousness. Every state developed case law on exploding bottle cases. In Los Angeles County, the largest, busiest trial court district in California, juries reached verdicts in an average of one to two exploding bottle cases a year during the mid-1950s.[12] Although the total number of civil cases tried to verdict during those years ranged from 383 in 1954 to 558 in 1957, and the vast majority of those cases were not product liability cases but personal injury cases of other kinds

---

[9]California Blue Book, 1950, 804.

[10]*Ibid.* at 787.

[11]Escola Court File, Brief for Respondent, March 24, 1943, 12.

[12]"Jury Verdict Chart of Los Angeles Recoveries, 1954–1957, republished from the Los Angeles Metropolitan News, April 22, 1958, in Melvin Belli, *Modern Trials,* Vol. IV (St. Paul, Minnesota, 1959), 220–22.

(most related to traffic accidents), exploding bottle cases were the most common product liability lawsuit.[13]

Manufacturers of consumer goods and their insurers were troubled by the advent of product liability lawsuits and even more so by the trend in jury awards to injured consumers.[14] In 1963 the national average for verdicts in product liability cases, $25,879, far exceeded the $11,473 average verdict for all types of personal injury cases.[15] And injured consumers had a better chance of winning than other personal injury plaintiffs. The overall personal injury plaintiff recovery rate was 53 percent, but consumers prevailed in 77 percent of their lawsuits against retailers, 73 percent of their lawsuits involving household products, and 62 percent of their lawsuits involving food or beverages.[16] As Belli noted, during the 1950s and 1960s, California, and particularly San Francisco, led the nation in the size of jury awards, and the frequency of large awards increased dramatically.[17] California produced more *res ipsa loquitur* product liability cases than any other state, putting it at the forefront not only of the rise of consumerism, but of the rise of product liability litigation.[18]

Insurance policies that specifically covered product liability had been available to the manufacturers, distributors, and sellers of consumer products since the 1920s.[19] By 1958 the insurance industry had developed a standardized policy covering legal obligations arising from death, injury, or property damage caused by an "accident" involving "goods or products manufactured, sold, handled or distributed by the named insured."[20] Insurance companies packaged product liability coverage with other commercial insurance and made it available in the

---

[13]*Ibid.* Also see William Night, "Let the Bottler Beware," *Insurance Counsel Journal* 21:72 (1954).

[14]Lester Dodd, "A Trial Attorney's Viewpoint of the Recent Trend Toward High Verdicts," *Insurance Counsel Journal* 19:369 (1952); Joseph Spray, "Current Trends in Jury Verdicts," *Insurance Counsel Journal* 20:109 (1953); and E. A. Cowie, "The Growing Cost of Tort Litigation and Its Significance to the Public and the Profession," *Insurance Counsel Journal* 26:590 (1959).

[15]Wallace Sedgwick, "Products Liability: Trial Problems in Warranty Cases," *Insurance Counsel Journal* 30: 616, 616 (1963).

[16]*Ibid.*

[17]Belli, *Modern Trials,* Vol. IV, 395, 819; Melvin Belli, *Modern Trials,* Vol. IV supplement (St. Paul, Minnesota, 1966).

[18]S. Burns Weston, "A Defense Lawyer Looks at Product Liability and *Res Ipsa Loquitur*," *Insurance Counsel Journal* 29: 576, 580 (1962).

[19]Suel O. Arnold, "Products Liability Insurance," *Insurance Counsel Journal* 25:42, 42 (1958).

[20]*Ibid.* at 45.

form of a "Comprehensive General Liability" or "Commercial Package."[21] By the early 1960s, insurance companies did a substantial business in product liability insurance. For instance, the Hartford insurance company took in about $2.5 million in premiums for product liability insurance in 1961.[22]

Surprisingly, the increasing frequency of product liability lawsuits and the trend in jury awards to consumers during the late 1950s and early 1960s did not initially cause an increase in insurance rates. "[D]espite the liberalization of recovery procedures," wrote Hartford insurance executive E. A. Cowie in 1962, "rates have not gone up for products liability protection for the past few years."[23] In fact, product liability insurance rates remained at the level prevailing in 1962, increasing only with inflation, until 1975.[24] Businesses paid increasing amounts for product liability insurance during the 1950s and 1960s not because rates increased, but because they bought insurance coverage for a higher volume and greater variety of products.[25] Although trends in product liability litigation troubled businesses and their insurers, the actual impact of this litigation on them paled in comparison with the transformative effects of the rise of a consumer economy.

The advent of the product liability lawsuit began to transform litigation practices. These cases were lucrative for the lawyers on both sides. Their increasing frequency and high verdicts meant more and higher fees for personal injury lawyers, like Melvin Belli, who were often paid on a contingency basis. Insurance defense lawyers also benefited. The amount of liability insurance claims during the 1950s increased at a far slower rate than the amount paid to defend against those claims.[26]

Product liability litigation was a growing area of legal practice. As a result, personal injury lawyers and insurance defense lawyers became more organized and more specialized. In 1945, 17 personal injury lawyers formed the National Association of Claimants Compensation Attorneys (the NACCA, since renamed the American Trial Lawyers Association), and the organization grew rapidly through the 1950s.[27] Although the NACCA created only a loose affiliation of

---

[21]Arnold, "Products Liability Insurance," 42, 42; Interagency Task Force on Product Liability, Product Liability: Final Report of the Insurance Study, Vol. 1, U.S. Department of Commerce (1977) ES-3.

[22]E. A. Cowie, *"Res Ipsa Loquitur* in Products Liability Actions: Insurance Company Viewpoint," *Insurance Counsel Journal* 29:583, 583 (1962).

[23]*Ibid.*

[24]Interagency Task Force on Product Liability, Product Liability: Final Report of the Insurance Study, Vol. 1, U.S Department of Commerce (1977) ES-4.

[25]Cowie, *"Res Ipsa Loquitur* in Products Liability Actions," 583, 583.

[26]E. A. Cowie, "The Growing Cost of Tort Litigation and Its Significance to the Public and the Profession," *Insurance Counsel Journal* 26:590, 590 (1959).

[27]H. Beale Rollins, "Industry's Answer to 'The More Adequate Award,'" *Insurance Counsel Journal* 21:455, 455 (1954).

independently operating lawyers who often had small general practices, it provided its members with data on particular products, past product liability cases, and industry standards. Perhaps most important, it helped plaintiffs' attorneys find experts to testify on technical issues that arose in product liability cases. The International Association of Insurance Counsel, formed in 1928, was somewhat more cohesive and consisted of an even more specialized group of lawyers. Like the NACCA, it provided its members with important data and expert referrals.

Gradually, product liability trials became complex, typically involving protracted legal battles between highly specialized lawyers backed by expert witnesses. Differences between the litigation in *Escola* and in *Greenman* illustrated the beginning of these trends in the practice of product liability law. In *Escola* the bottling company called two expert witnesses on the physics of exploding bottles, but the trial still took only a day. The *Greenman* trial lasted several days and was dominated by the technical testimony of experts on both sides. In contrast to *Escola* and *Greenman,* product liability cases today often take weeks or months to try. These cases often involve complex litigation and go before a jury only after protracted legal wrangling over pretrial discovery. The complexity of the litigation and the technical nature of the subject matter pushed personal injury lawyers toward increasingly narrow fields of specialization.

In the early days of the product liability lawsuit, trial judges had great influence over trial outcomes. At the time of the *Escola* trial, standardized jury instructions, written and published by a committee of Los Angeles County Superior Court Judges, were just beginning to come into use. The Committee on Standard Jury Instructions published its first edition of standard civil jury instructions in 1938. However, the trial judge in *Escola* explained *res ipsa loquitur* to the jury in his own words, and his explanation favored Gladys Escola.[28] Between *Escola* and *Greenman* the Court heard several product liability cases that involved *res ipsa loquitur.* Judging from these cases, trial judges often gave the

---

[28]The following are two of the instructions the judge read the jury in Escola:

"In the case before you, it is the claim of plaintiff that a bottle of defendant's Coca Cola exploded and injured her hand. While under our law the burden is on the plaintiff to prove all of the affirmative allegations of her complaint, the reasonable inferences to be drawn from the evidence adduced are left to your fair and rational judgment as triers of facts. If you were satisfied from the evidence that it contained a reasonable inference that said bottle of Coca Cola did explode and did injure plaintiff, this will be a legal basis upon which a verdict for the plaintiff may be supported." Escola Court File, Opening Statement of Melvin Belli, Reporter's Transcript on Appeal, 92.

"If it is shown you that the injury in question arose out of the explosion of a bottle of defendant's Coca Cola, under the circumstances as outlined above, our law then raises a presumption or inference of negligence attaching itself to the defendants, and the burden of proof is then case upon the defendants to free themselves from charge." Escola Court File, Opening Statement by Melvin Belli, Reporter's Transcript on Appeal, 97.

jury nonstandard or "tailored" instructions on the doctrine over the objection of the defendant.[29] Judges' strongly worded instructions in previous cases often belied a view of those cases sympathetic to the injured consumer. By the time of the *Greenman* trial in 1960, the use of standardized jury instructions had become much more common. Greenman's attorneys requested "tailored" jury instructions that favored their client, but the judge gave only the standard jury instructions. The use of standardized jury instructions reduced the influence of trial judges.

Trial judges exercised broad discretion in deciding the law that applied to product liability cases. In exploding bottle cases, like *Escola,* they decided whether to instruct the jury on *res ipsa loquitur.* Nothing required them to instruct juries on that doctrine. To the contrary, prior to *Escola* some California case law held the doctrine to be inapplicable where a beverage bottle had passed from the bottler into the hands of others and then exploded, causing an injury.[30] As Belli noted to the Court in his *Escola* brief, however, trial courts had frequently instructed juries on *res ipsa loquitur* in exploding bottle cases. "Without the use of the doctrine," he wrote, "plaintiff could never prevail in these cases, no matter how justifiable his or her claim would be."[31] Although most of these exploding bottle cases did not reach the California Supreme Court, the trial practices in these cases delineated the issues that ultimately came before the Court.

The Trend Toward Strict Liability

Belli referred to Traynor's opinion in *Escola* as the beginning of a "tort revolution," and it did constitute a significant break with legal precedent.[32] However, earlier doctrinal changes in cases involving product warranties prepared the way for *Escola,* and Traynor himself alluded to these changes. He contended that strict liability was the logical extension of warranty cases, and he cited cases ruling that "implied warranties of fitness for proposed use and merchantable quality include a warranty of safety of the product."[33] Warranty theory circumvented issues involving the proof of negligence, but it also created an obstacle for the injured consumer—the doctrine of "privity of contract." Historically, the

---

[29]See e.g., Gordon v. Aztec Brewing Co., 33 Cal.2d 514, 519 (1949); Peterson v. Lamb Rubber, 54 Cal.2d 339, 348 (1960).

[30]Gerber v. Faber, 54 Cal.App.2d 674, 684 (1942). It is interesting to note that Rey Schauer, Presiding Judge of the Second District of the Court of Appeals, concurred with this opinion, but, two years later, after he had been elevated to the Supreme Court, he concurred with the majority in Escola.

[31]Escola Court File, Brief for Respondent, March 24, 1943, 10.

[32]Belli, ed., *Trial and Tort Trends, 1964–65 Seminar,* 3.

[33]Escola, 24 Cal.2d at 464.

"privity of contract" requirement meant that an injured person had to have dealt directly with a manufacturer in order to recover money from the manufacturer for injuries caused by the manufacturer's product. As in contract cases generally, legal obligations in warranty cases depended on contractual relations between the parties.

Several courts found ways to circumvent the "privity of contract" requirement. In 1916 Judge Benjamin Cardozo's landmark decision *McPherson v. Buick Motor Co.* held that a manufacturer was liable for injuries caused by its products during the proper use of those products by a foreseeable user.[34] The case involved a car with defective wood wheels that crumbled, causing injury to the owner, McPherson, who had bought the car from a dealer, not from the manufacturer, Buick. Although McPherson was not "in privity" with Buick, Cardozo held he could recover his losses from the manufacturer. Following *McPherson,* other courts moved to limit or abolish the "privity of contract" requirement in warranty cases. In the 1960 New Jersey Supreme Court case of *Henningsen v. Bloomfield Motors, Inc.,* the Court upheld a verdict for a woman who was injured by a defective car her husband had bought, even though she was not "in privity" with the negligent manufacturer.[35] Traynor cited *Henningsen* and other cases that demonstrated the erosion of the "privity of contract" requirement as support for his position that the law was moving toward a strict liability standard in defective product cases. However, in 1963, when Traynor decided *Greenman,* most courts continued to require privity of contract.[36]

Traynor made a historical argument designed to eliminate any vestiges of the "privity of contract" requirement. "Warranties are not necessarily rights arising out of contract." he wrote, "an action on a warranty 'was, in its origin, a pure action of tort,' and only late in the historical development of warranties was an action in assumpsit allowed."[37] In other words, the original law of warranties provided precedent for a consumer to recover money for a civil wrong committed by a producer even when the consumer and the producer had no contractual relations. Despite the questionable accuracy of Traynor's historical interpretation, it enabled him to point out the transitory nature of legal precedent while, at the same time, claiming some legal authority for his position.[38]

Traynor's opinion in *Escola* set forth three primary arguments for making manufacturers carry the costs of consumer injuries caused by defective products.

---

[34]McPherson v. Buick Motor Co., 217 N.Y. 382 (1916).

[35]Henningsen, 161 A.2d 69.

[36]See G. Edward White, *Tort Law in America: An Intellectual History* (New York, 1980), 168.

[37]Escola, 24 Cal.2d at 466. It is interesting to note that William Prosser made the same argument in *Handbook of the Law of Torts.* See note 43 *infra* at 690.

[38]See Holmes, *The Common Law,* 205

First, a strict liability standard would deter some potentially injurious product defects. "It is to the public interest to discourage the marketing of products having defects that are a menace to the public," Traynor wrote.[39] Second, a strict liability standard would shift the costs of injuries caused by defective products to manufacturers who were better able to insure against the risk of those injuries. "If such [defective] products . . . find their way into the market," Traynor wrote,

> it is to the public interest to place the responsibility for whatever injury they may cause upon the manufacturer, who, even if he is not negligent in the manufacture of the product, is responsible for its reaching the market. . . . Against such a risk there should be general and constant protection and the manufacturer is best situated to afford such protection.[40]

Third, a strict liability standard would relieve those injured by defective products of the unreasonable and unfair legal burden of proving the cause of the defect. "An injured person . . . is not ordinarily in a position to refute such evidence or identify the cause of the defect," Traynor wrote, "for he can hardly be familiar with the manufacturing process as the manufacturer himself is."[41] The underlying objective of each of Traynor's policy arguments was the protection of individual consumers.

Traynor cited numerous law review articles and other untraditional legal authorities in *Escola*,[42] but his opinion most closely resembled the argument in William Prosser's 1941 treatise *The Law of Torts*.[43] Traynor cited Prosser's treatise in his *Escola* opinion, and both men contended that strict liability would make good social policy. They cited the same scholarly articles in their work and argued by analogy to statutes dealing with adulterated food. Traynor knew Prosser, the preeminent tort scholar of his day, and the two men had a cordial professional relationship. In 1947, Boalt Hall asked Traynor to assist in the search for a new dean. Traynor recommended three men, and the school chose Prosser from that group.[44] Traynor later sat on Prosser's committee on the Re-

---

[39]Escola, 24 Cal.2d at 462.

[40]*Ibid.*

[41]*Ibid.,* 463.

[42]Traynor cited William Prosser, "The Implied Warranty of Merchantable Quality, *Minnesota Law Review* 27:117 (1943); Robert C. Brown, "The Liability of Retail Dealers for Defective Food Products, *Minnesota Law Review* 23:585 (1939); John Barker Waite, "Retail Responsibility and Judicial Law Making, *Michigan Law Review* 34:494 (1936); and Karl Llewellyn, "On Warranty of Quality and Society, *Columbia Law Review* 36:699 (1936).

[43]William Prosser, *Handbook of the Law of Torts* (St. Paul, Minnesota, 1941), 688–93.

[44]Epstein, "Law at Berkeley," 276.

statement (Second) of Torts.[45] As Traynor's chief staff attorney Don Barrett noted, Traynor's decision in *Escola* reflected Prosser's influence.[46]

G. Edward White has argued that the "dominant theories of tort law can be identified with the theories of a small but influential group of persons."[47] White asserted that a group of legal scholars heavily influenced Traynor's thinking. However, Traynor arrived at his position on strict liability well before the subject generated much scholarly interest. Aside from Prosser, few scholars took up the subject before 1944, when Traynor wrote his concurrence in *Escola*. None of the 15 law review articles Traynor cited in that opinion called for the adoption of a strict liability standard in product liability cases. Only during the 1950s and 1960s, well after Traynor had formed his views on the subject, did the adoption of strict liability gain much scholarly attention.

Traynor was certainly aware of the growing scholarly interest in tort reform. However, as Prosser observed in his widely influential 1960 article "The Assault Upon the Citadel (Strict Liability to the Consumer)," the movement for strict liability originated with agitation over adulterated food, not with the academy's desire for reform.[48] Prosser described a "prolonged and violent national agitation over defective food, which at times almost reached national hysteria."[49] By 1960, 17 states had adopted a strict liability standard in adulterated food cases.[50] Prosser's *Restatement (Second) of Torts* tentative draft number 7, issued in 1962, also called for strict liability in adulterated food cases (but not in defective product cases).[51] Although Prosser and a few other legal scholars became outspoken advocates for tort reform, the trend toward strict liability reflected more widespread changes in attitudes toward product liability cases. Tort reform was not just the concern of a few influential academics, it was a matter of growing societal interest.

The Court's Movement from *Escola* to *Greenman*

The product liability cases that reached the Court between *Escola* and *Greenman* turned on the issue of whether an injured consumer could recover under the *res ipsa loquitur* doctrine. A crucial legal question in those cases was whether

[45]Interview with Don Barrett by Ben Field, May 24, 1997.

[46]*Ibid.*

[47]White, *Tort Law in America,* xii.

[48]William Prosser, "The Assault Upon the Citadel (Strict Liability to the Consumer)," *Yale Law Journal* 69:1099, 1144–45 (1960).

[49]*Ibid.*

[50]*Ibid.* at 1107–10.

[51]Restatement (Second) Torts, section 402(a), Comment "J," tentative draft number 7 (1962).

the defendant had "exclusive control" of the product that caused the injury; the *res ipsa loquitur* doctrine required proof that the defendant had "exclusive control." Beginning with *Escola,* the Court expanded the concept of "exclusive control" to accommodate consumers injured by exploding bottles. The Court's application of *res ipsa loquitur* seemed strained, even to Traynor. Ultimately, the strain on the doctrine stimulated a reevaluation of the field and the consideration of other doctrinal schemes for product liability.

By the time the Court decided *Greenman,* Traynor had repeatedly urged his brethren to reject *res ipsa loquitur* and warranty doctrine as the principal theories of product liability. In the 1949 case of *Gordon v. Aztec Brewing Company,* a bartender had lost sight in one eye when an Aztec Brewing Company beer bottle exploded in his hand.[52] The majority upheld the judgment for the bartender and against the bottler, citing its decision in *Escola* on *res ipsa loquitur,* but the majority expanded that concept too much for Traynor. Traynor found that *res ipsa loquitur* could not apply because the defect in the exploding bottle could have been caused after the bottle left the bottler's hands and, therefore, the bottler did not have "exclusive control" of the bottle.[53] The majority had expanded *res ipsa loquitur* to the point where "exclusive control" began to lose its meaning. Traynor wrote a concurring opinion, joined by no other justice, in which he argued that the bottler should be held responsible for defects that resulted "from normal marketing procedures" after the bottle left the bottler's control even though *res ipsa loquitur* did not apply. He contended that the public interest in discouraging "the marketing of products having defects that are a menace to the public" justified the adoption of a strict liability standard.[54]

In 1958 the California Supreme Court heard the case of Ruth Trust, who suffered an injury to her wrist when a bottle of skim milk broke as she set it on her kitchen drainboard.[55] Trust sued the Owens-Illinois Glass Company, which manufactured the bottle, and Arden Farms, which filled the bottle with milk. Traynor again argued that a bottler (this time a milk bottler) should be held strictly liable for an injury caused by its defective bottle.[56] His opinion traced the Court's efforts to apply traditional negligence doctrine in cases involving defective food containers. Noting that a strict liability standard already applied to food products, Traynor argued, "there is no rational basis for differentiating between foodstuffs and their containers."[57] He used the doctrinal instability of product liability law to move the court toward a liability standard he considered more coherent and functional.

---

[52]Gordon, 33 Cal.2d 514.

[53]*Ibid.*

[54]*Ibid.,* 531.

[55]Trust v. Arden Farms Co., 50 Cal.2d 217 (1958).

[56]*Ibid.*

[57]*Ibid.,* 237.

Incremental changes gradually undermined established product liability doctrine. The language of the court's majority opinion in the 1960 case of *Peterson v. Lamb Rubber Co.* pushed that doctrine to the breaking point.[58] The case involved a worker who lost the sight in his left eye when a grinding wheel, which the manufacturer had sold to his employer, "blew up" in his face. By traditional standards, Peterson, the worker, and Lamb Rubber, the manufacturer, were not in privity of contract. Justice Schauer, writing for the whole Court except Traynor, avoided this legal obstacle by considering employees "members of the industrial 'family' of the employer."[59] Traynor agreed that Peterson should be allowed to recover his losses from Lamb Rubber, but only for the reasons he had given in *Escola* and *Gordon*. Although none of his brethren joined in his opinion, their "industrial family" language proved to be the final incremental change in product liability law before its overhaul in *Greenman*.

Traynor went out of his way to consider the virtues of strict liability while the parties and his brethren repeatedly disregarded them. Since no case law directly supported his views, Traynor made arguments based on analogy and analysis of the historical development of product liability doctrine. In *Escola,* he pointed out that the California Health and Safety Code criminalizing the manufacture, packing, advertising, and sales of adulterated foods imposed a rule of strict liability. He argued by analogy that the same standard should apply to the manufacture of defective products.[60] Traynor did not cite any case in which a court imposed strict liability on a manufacturer of a defective product because no such precedent existed.

One of the clearest indications that strict liability was a theory without much contemporary legal precedent was that litigants did not argue the theory. In *Escola* the parties devoted all their attention to the question of whether the doctrine of *res ipsa loquitur* applied in exploding bottle cases. Escola's lawyers contended the question had not previously been decided by the Court, but pointed out that plaintiff's lawyers commonly used *res ipsa loquitur* in exploding bottle cases at the trial court level.[61] If a plaintiff's lawyer in a product liability case could convince a trial judge that the doctrine might apply, the judge would instruct the jury on the doctrine. The jury then would have a vehicle for finding the manufacturer liable. The elasticity of the *res ipsa loquitur* doctrine enabled trial courts to accommodate litigants who suffered injuries from defective products.

Traynor and the *Escola* lawyers shared a preference for rules of liability that favored the interests of individuals injured by defective products over the inter-

---

[58] Peterson, 54 Cal.2d 339.

[59] *Ibid.,* 347.

[60] Escola, 24 Cal.2d at 463. Traynor made this argument in Trust and Greenman as well.

[61] Escola Court File, Respondent's Brief, March 24, 1943, 10.

ests of manufacturers of consumer goods. Citing a law review article and cases from other state courts, Escola's lawyers asserted briefly that for public policy reasons manufacturers should insure themselves against the risk of exploding bottles.[62] Traynor agreed that consumer injuries were not just a matter of "private law," but a societal problem best addressed as a matter of public policy. He agreed that for public policy reasons the responsibility to insure against the risk of consumer injuries ought to be shifted from consumers to manufacturers. Beyond these basic similarities, however, Traynor's opinion bore little resemblance to the arguments of the litigants. His opinion consisted of a policy analysis developed independently of the lawyers' arguments.

In *Greenman* the questions disputed by the parties had even less to do with strict liability. The attorneys for Yuba Power Products contended that Greenman had not met the requirement to notify Yuba of his warranty claim within a reasonable period of time. *California Civil Code* section 1769 stated that a seller who did not receive from a buyer notice of a warranty claim "within a reasonable time after the buyer knows, or ought to know of such breach . . . shall not be liable therefor."[63] Yuba's attorneys sought a reversal of the verdict on the grounds that the jury should not have been instructed on breach of warranty because Greenman waited almost 11 months to notify Yuba of his claim. Greenman's attorneys argued the other side of the same issue. Neither side made an argument concerning strict liability. As in *Escola*, Traynor's opinion drew little on the lawyers' arguments.

The California Supreme Court's adoption of Traynor's theory of strict liability in *Greenman* came about in part because the Court's membership had changed and in part because the senior justices changed their positions. In 1963, when the Court unanimously decided *Greenman*, three justices, Raymond Peters, Mathew Tobriner, and Paul Peek, had recently been appointed to the Court by Governor Pat Brown.[64] Although Peters had joined the Court in time to concur in *Peterson*, the "industrial family" decision, none of the three had much of a record on product liability cases. Of the remaining three justices who decided *Greenman*, two, Chief Justice Gibson and Justice Schauer, had been on the Court when it decided *Escola* 19 years earlier; Chief Justice Gibson wrote the majority opinion in which Justice Schauer joined. The third, Justice McComb wrote the majority opinion in *Trust*, the milk bottle case, affirming the judgment in favor of the dairy and glass manufacturer. Prior to voting with Traynor in *Greenman*, these judges disagreed with Traynor's position on the need to adopt a strict liability standard.

---

[62]*Ibid.* at 13.

[63]California Civil Code section 1769 as quoted in Greenman, 59 Cal.2d at 60.

[64]Peters joined the court in 1959. Tobriner and Peek joined in 1962. Johnson, *History of the Supreme Court Justices of California*, 3.

Traynor consistently advocated the same position on strict liability during the 19 years between *Escola* and *Greenman*. He repeatedly encouraged the Court to discontinue its reliance on the legal "fictions" built into the *res ipsa loquitur* and warranty doctrines.[65] Juries, he argued, were left "free to impose strict liability if they so choose, under the guise of *res ipsa loquitur*."[66] The concept of privity of contract, embedded in warranty doctrine, was "needlessly circuitous and [it] engenders wasteful litigation."[67] Traynor contended that the Court's continued disregard of the conceptual shortcomings of conventional product liability law reflected badly on the Court.

Although the Court repeatedly rejected Traynor's calls for the adoption of a strict liability standard, its willingness to stretch the doctrines of *res ipsa loquitur* and privity of contract signaled the gradual erosion of the traditional scheme of product liability. With increasing frequency, plaintiffs' lawyers took advantage of this gradual doctrinal erosion. During a three-month period in early 1963 more product warranty cases went to trial than during the two previous years.[68] The Court's adoption of the "industrial family" fiction in *Peterson* marked the culmination of incremental doctrinal change that supplanted the concept of privity under the guise of retaining it. The disintegration of consensus on the Court in support of applying traditional doctrines to product liability cases created an opening for Traynor's justification for reform.

The Political Economy of Tort Reform

Traynor's opinion in *Escola* included a discussion of contemporary market conditions that were atypical of judicial opinions. He expressed concern about the power disparity between manufacturers and consumers. "As handicrafts have been replaced by mass production with its great markets and transportation facilities," he noted,

> the close relationship between the producer and consumer of a product has been altered. Manufacturing processes, frequently valuable secrets, are ordinarily either inaccessible to or beyond the ken of the general public. The consumer no longer has means or skill enough to investigate for himself the soundness of a product, even when it is not contained in a sealed package, and his erstwhile vigilance has been lulled by the steady efforts of manufacturers to build up confidence by advertising and marketing devices. . . . Consumers no longer ap-

---

[65] Escola, 24 Cal.2d at 465; Trust, 50 Cal.2d at 236–37; Gordon, 33 Cal.2d at 532.
[66] Trust, 50 Cal.2d at 237.
[67] Escola, 24 Cal.2d at 464.
[68] Sedgwick, "Products Liability," 616, 616.

proach products warily but accept them on faith, relying on the reputation of the manufacturer or the trade mark.[69]

Traynor saw consumers as relatively powerless to protect themselves against defective products. Producers, on the other hand, wielded great power in the marketplace. While consumers injured by defective products had no adequate means of informing the marketplace of their injury, manufacturers controlled virtually all the sources of information about their products available to consumers. Certainly, Traynor's contemporaries on the bench recognized the dramatic changes that came with the rise of mass marketing, but Traynor, more than other judges, identified them as a reason for legal reform.

The rhetoric of Traynor's product liability opinions suggested the assumptions, preferences, and aversions that underlay his rationale for reform. The use of particular words in a judicial opinion does not always illuminate the thinking of the judge who authored the opinion. Many judges, including Traynor, used clerks and staff attorneys to draft opinions. According to Don Barrett, he himself drafted Traynor's opinion in *Greenman*,[70] and a law clerk assisted with Traynor's opinion in *Escola*.[71] However, Traynor carefully reviewed the word selection in any draft produced by a clerk, so some conclusions can be drawn from Traynor's rhetoric of policy analysis.[72]

Unlike Chief Justice Phil Gibson, another progressive judge, Traynor used the word "plaintiff" in *Escola* only once. Instead, Traynor's extensive discussion of the economic context of product liability law referred to "consumers" 12 times. He analyzed the allocation of the "cost" of defective products and the salutary effect of a rule requiring manufacturers to insure themselves against the "risk" of injuries caused by their defective products. His opinions in product liability cases, particularly *Escola,* placed "public policy" and "public interest" at the center of his legal discourse. He replaced the standard legal terminology of tort cases—the language of blame—with the language of policy analysis.

For Traynor product liability law was a form of public policy. He used the phrases "public policy" or "public interest" nine times in his *Escola* opinion and five times in his *Gordon* opinion. His argument in *Escola* consisted mainly of an analysis of policy objectives and the means to achieve those objectives. Traynor recognized injuries caused by product defects as social costs of a consumer economy, and he treated product liability law as a system for allocating those

---

[69]*Ibid.,* 467.

[70]Interview with Don Barrett by Ben Field, May 24, 1997.

[71]*Ibid.*

[72]In an October 5, 1998, interview, John Junker, one of Traynor's clerks in 1962–63, recollected Traynor's careful word selection. Junker drafted an opinion in which his summary of the facts of the case stated that one of the parties had flown out of state. Traynor crossed out the word "flown" and replaced it with "went by plane."

costs. For that reason his product liability opinions lacked the traditional judicial emphasis on the allocation of blame to the parties. "[P]ublic policy demands that responsibility be fixed wherever it will most effectively reduce the hazards to life and health inherent in defective products that reach the market," he wrote in *Escola.*[73]

With the rise of consumerism, Americans brought more and more products into their lives without knowing much about those products, aside from what they had learned from marketing and advertising. Traynor's conception of public interest recognized the pervasive, but often hidden, risks to consumers built into the new economic circumstances of life. "The manufacturer's obligation to the consumer must keep pace with the changing relationship between them," he wrote in *Escola.*[74] Strict liability to the consumer was Traynor's response to the new relationship between buyers and sellers in the marketplace that came with the rise of mass marketing and mass consumption.

Like many liberal policymakers of his time, Traynor exhibited ambivalence toward big business. But instead of seeking to penalize business his solution to the problem of consumer injuries caused by defective products spread the costs of the injuries. He sought to change the rules of product liability so that consumers would be insured against the risk of injuries caused by defective products. He recognized that product liability insurance was available to manufacturers but not readily available to consumers, and he believed that "public policy requires that the buyer be insured at the seller's expense against injury."[75] The manufacturer was to carry the cost of insurance for reasons of economic efficiency. Ultimately, this cost would be "distributed among the public as a cost of doing business."[76] Traynor thus saw strict liability as necessary to correct marketplace failings, not as a penalty against manufacturers. He even credited manufacturers with seeking "to justify that [consumer] faith by increasingly high standards of inspection and readiness to make good on defective products by way of replacement and refunds."[77] However, he also discussed the manufacturers' "responsibility"—not just their liability—as if manufacturers bore a moral obligation to consumers, not just a legal one.[78] Although Traynor's product liability opinions generally used the neutral sounding rhetoric of policy analysis, his sympathies lay with the injured consumer.

Traynor's opinions in cases involving business reflected the view that business could take care of itself. For instance, he was disinclined to use the power of the court to aid business in labor disputes. In the 1960 case of *Messner v.*

---

[73]Escola, 24 Cal.2d at 462.
[74]*Ibid.*
[75]*Ibid.,* 464.
[76]*Ibid.,* 462.
[77]*Ibid.,* 467.
[78]*Ibid.,* 463.

Journeymen Barbers, Justice Rey Schauer wrote in dissent that the "new majority" (referring to Traynor, Gibson, Torbiner, Peters, and Peck) had undertaken
an "ambitious project" to expand organized labor's power to unionize work-
places.[79] In *Messner,* Traynor, Chief Justice Gibson, and Justices White and
Peters reversed an injunction against the picketing of a barbershop intended to
force a closed or union shop agreement on the owner and his employees.[80]
Traynor's opinion went beyond the interpretation of legal precedent; he offered
a general justification for his *laissez-faire* approach toward labor activities.
Ironically, Traynor's language echoed the sentiments of the opponents of his
own innovative decisions:

> [The Court] felt bound to respect the traditional principle of separation of pow-
> ers that gives to the Legislature the responsibility of making any major changes
> in social and economic policy. It made clear that the court would not establish
> by judicial legislation a little Taft-Hartley Act for California that only the Leg-
> islature can properly consider and enact. The Legislature is uniquely able to
> amass economic data and hold hearings where it can give heed to many repre-
> sentatives of the public besides parties to a controversy. It can best determine
> whether there should be further governmental regulation of peaceful competi-
> tive economic activity.[81]

Like the opponents of his own activist decisions, Traynor employed arguments supporting the prerogative of the legislature, and he posited that the legislature's fact-finding capabilities made it better able to fashion good policy. Although Traynor was often accused of legislating from the bench, his language in
Messner showed his aversion to "judicial legislation" that constrained labor activities.

In contests like *Messner,* involving organized economic interests, where
Traynor saw no great disparity in power, he deferred to the legislature.[82] Traynor
did not always favor the less economically powerful party in cases where there
was a manifest disparity of power. To the contrary, in eminent domain cases
pitting small landowners against government entities that sought to use land for
some public purpose, Traynor generally favored the government.[83] In those

---

[79]Messner v. Journeymen Barbers, 53 Cal.2d 873, 890 (1960).
[80]*Ibid.*
[81]*Ibid.,* 882.
[82]See also Petri Cleaners, Inc. v. Automotive Employees, etc., Local 88, 53 Cal.2d
455 (1960).
[83]See e.g., Bacich v. Board of Control of the State of California, 23 Cal.2d 343
(1943); Miramar Co. v. City of Santa Barbara, 23 Cal.2d 170 (1943); City of Whittier v.
Dixon, 24 Cal.2d 664 (1944); Holloway v. Purcell, 35 Cal.2d 220 (1950); and People ex
Rel. Department of Public Works v. Superior Court of Merced (Rodoni), 68 Cal.2d 206
(1968).

cases, his approach was that of the anti-activist. He tended to operate legalistically, kept his reasoning close to precedent, and eschewed policy-based analysis.

In Traynor's view, consumers in product liability cases occupied a unique position because their powerlessness coincided with a strong public interest in protecting them. This unique position justified Traynor in his attempts to advance strict liability as the standard in product defect cases. Traynor often did not favor plaintiffs in other sorts of tort cases. He repeatedly refused to apply strict liability in cases that did not involve a defective product, even where the defendant was a business.[84] He refused to extend strict liability to property owners for injuries caused on their property.[85] In cases where visitors sued property owners for injuries that occurred on the property owners' property and where both had the same information about the danger of the premises, Traynor generally ruled against the injured visitors. Unlike the consumer, the injured visitor was not unknowingly exposed to a risk of injury along with many other people; Traynor saw them as individually responsible for their actions and the injuries they suffered as a result.

In keeping with his general preference for spreading the costs of injuries caused by defective products, Traynor generally favored expansive Workmen's Compensation coverage.[86] In the infamous case of *Wiseman v. Industrial Accident Commission,* Traynor awarded Workmen's Compensation death benefits to a widow and daughter of a banker who died on a business trip to New York City.[87] After a night of drinking, the bed Wiseman shared with another woman caught fire—presumably because of a cigarette. Although the risk of death by fire during an adulterous tryst was not a widespread occupational hazard, Traynor found it to be work-related because Wiseman was on a business trip. The basic purpose of Workmen's Compensation was the promotion of economic security through the distribution of job-related risks. While Traynor emphasized individual responsibility in many tort cases, he believed society should insure individuals against the risk of injury when the individual was participating in the economy as a consumer or as a worker.

---

[84]See e.g., Neel v. Mannings, Inc., 19 Cal.2d 647 (1942) (dissenting opinion); Blumberg v. M. and T. Inc, 34 Cal.2d 226 (1949) (dissenting opinion); Laird v. T. W. Mather, Inc., 51 Cal.2d 210 (1958).

[85]See e.g., Neel, 19 Cal.2d 647 (dissenting opinion); Blumberg, 34 Cal.2d 226 (dissenting opinion); Devens v. Goldberg 33 Cal.2d 173 (1948) (dissenting opinion); Knight v. Kaiser Co., 48 Cal.2d 778 (1957) (dissenting opinion); Laird, 51 Cal.2d 210; and Rowland v. Christian, 69 Cal.2d 108 (1968).

[86]See e.g., California Casualty Indemnity Exchange v. Industrial Accident Commission, 21 Cal.2d 461 (1942); Argonaut Insurance Co. v. Industrial Accident Commission, 57 Cal.2d 589 (1962); California Compensation and Fire Co. v. Industrial Accident Commission, 57 Cal.2d 598 (1962).

[87]Wiseman v. Industrial Accident Commission, 46 Cal.2d 570 (1956).

A dominant theme of the New Deal and post-New Deal periods was the need to promote economic security through social insurance, and Traynor's strict liability opinions echoed that theme. As he wrote in *Escola,* "the cost of an injury and the loss of time or health may be an overwhelming misfortune to the person injured, and a needless one, for the risk of injury can be insured by the manufacturer and distributed among the public as a cost of doing business."[88] Traynor analogized product liability insurance to social insurance, citing Harvard Law School Dean Roscoe Pound's argument connecting the two. "Today there is a strong and growing tendency to revive the idea of liability without fault," Pound had written,

> not only in a form of wide responsibility for agencies employed, but in placing upon an enterprise the burden of repairing injuries without fault of him who conducts it, which are incident to the undertaking. There is a strong and growing tendency, where there is no blame on either side, to ask, in view of the exigencies of social justice, who can best bear the loss, and hence to shift the loss by creating liability where there has been no fault.[89]

Although he employed the language of tort law, Pound's argument dealt more broadly with all forms of public policy, particularly Workmen's Compensation, which redistributed the costs of injury inherent in economic activity. Traynor, like Pound, believed that the policy objectives of tort law and Workmen's Compensation converged to the extent that both might redistribute certain intrinsic risks of modern economic activity.

California Supreme Court Justice Mathew Tobriner, who joined in the *Greenman* opinion, referred to that decision as "an affirmation of individualism."[90] By repositioning and spreading the risks to the consumer of the modern marketplace, *Greenman* helped give consumers security from economic catastrophe. The pursuit of economic security was a theme that reverberated through the New Deal and post-New Deal eras. As FDR explained in his Four Freedoms Speech, "individual freedom cannot exist without economic security and independence."[91] Ideological change during the New Deal and post-New Deal eras connected product liability reforms with this desire for economic freedom. Strict liability reflected a shift in American individualism away from the notion of individual responsibility embodied in the rule "let the buyer beware" and toward an emphasis on freedom to consume. As the International Association of Insurance Counsel noted in its 1955 report,

---

[88]*Escola,* 24 Cal.2d at 462.

[89]Roscoe Pound, "The End of Law as Developed in Legal Rules and Doctrines," *Harvard Law Review* 27:195 233 (1914) cited in *Escola,* 24 Cal.2d at 466.

[90]Mathew Tobriner, "Lawyers, Judges, and Watergate," *Journal of the State Bar* 49:116 (1974).

[91]*Ibid.* at 386.

There is a growing tendency among the courts and writers to seek to make the manufacturer liable in these cases regardless of the arguments concerning privity of contract. . . . This change in concept of the law can be traced directly to our changing political philosophy and theory of protecting the general public through social security and other legislative measures.[92]

Greenman helped safeguard the sense of self-fulfillment and material security that came with product consumption. It advanced individual freedom by ensuring the economic security and financial independence essential to freedom. To the extent that product consumption expressed individualism, *Greenman* promoted the expression of individual choice as well.

The Reaction to Traynor's Strict Liability Doctrine

Greenman was a landmark in the massive shift in judicial thinking toward strict liability. Before *Greenman,* courts used various artifices to allow consumers to gain compensation for injuries caused by defective products,[93] and strict liability doctrine received little attention from judges. State courts outside California cited Traynor's *Escola* concurrence only twice before *Greenman.*[94] Only after *Greenman* did courts frequently cite Traynor's *Escola* concurrence with approval. Indeed, after 1963, state courts outside of California cited it approvingly 60 times. As for *Greenman* itself, state courts outside of California cited the decision in 280 opinions. These cases often referred to *Greenman* as a "seminal" or a "landmark" product liability case, and they often mentioned Traynor by name. Many of these cases also noted the widespread influence of Traynor's

---

[92]Ray Andersen, "Current Problems in Products Liability Law and Products Liability Insurance," *Insurance Counsel Journal* 31:436, 436 (1964). One member of the International Association of Insurance Counsel Executive Committee, Wallace Sedgwick, was even more explicit: "[T]hese developments in personal injury-liability in the products field," he wrote, "reflect sweeping changes in political philosophy in this country in the last Century, particularly since the great depression of 1929. In the political field these changes have resulted in the acceptance by a majority of our people of the principle that economic vicissitudes are not the inevitable plight of the average individual, and that it is the function of the state to come to the aid of the citizen in such instances. Social security, employment insurance, and other programs of the so-called 'Welfare State' are the obvious examples." Sedgwick, "Products Liability," 616, 626.

[93]See Cornelius Gillam, "Products Liability in a Nutshell," *Oregon Law Review* 37:119, 153–55 (1957).

[94]The Municipal Court of the City of New York noted that Traynor's strict liability doctrine avoided a "needlessly circuitous" legal process. Parish v. A. and P., 177 N.Y.S.2d 7 (1958). The Nevada Supreme Court referred to Traynor's concurrence as "extreme." Underhill v. Anciaux 226 P.2d 794, 796 (1951).

thinking. Within three years of *Greenman* the courts of 18 states had adopted strict liability for manufacturers in product liability cases.[95]

Many courts outside of California made public policy arguments for strict liability based largely on the language of *Greenman* and *Escola*. Their discussions of the efficiency of shifting the economic burden of injuries caused by defective products, the creation of an economic disincentive for manufacturers to cause consumer injuries, and the need to relieve consumers of the burden of proof in product liability cases drew most often from Traynor's opinions. After the Restatement (Second) of Torts in 1965, courts added the Restatement and law review articles by Prosser as sources of the public policy rationale for strict liability, but courts continued to refer to Traynor's thinking as the genesis of the movement toward strict liability.

Despite the magnitude of the changes in product liability law, the public reacted to *Escola* and *Greenman* with indifference. Few people outside the legal community knew of these cases. Neither case generated even a mention in a major California newspaper. Product liability reform had no noticeable effect on the cost of consumer goods so consumers did not see signs of the change. Although manufacturers passed on the cost of product liability insurance to consumers, insurance rates increased little in the years immediately preceding and following *Greenman,* despite the trend of liberalized recovery.[96] This price stability made consumer dissatisfaction unlikely.

Industry responses to changes in product liability law were mixed. On one hand, numerous lawyers who practiced insurance defense wrote in embattled tones of trends in product liability law, often demonizing Melvin Belli and the NACCA. In rhetorical response to the NACCA's assault on the citadel of privity, some insurance defense lawyers called on their colleagues to "man the bastions."[97] However, not all in the insurance industry were so alarmed. One insurance company executive wrote in 1962,

> I am not greatly offended by some of the changes in the law of products liability and particularly those eliminating or lessening the classical requirement of privity of contract. . . . My associates and I are not particularly surprised nor horrified at what is happening. It makes sense to me in some cases that a manufacturer should be required to explain the composition of his product and the

---

[95]William Prosser, "The Fall of the Citadel (Strict Liability to the Consumer)," *Minnesota Law Review* 50:791 (1966).

[96]Cowie, *"Res Ipsa Loquitur,"* 583, 583.

[97]See e.g., Wallace Sedgwick, "Current Trends in Products Liability Field," *Insurance Counsel Journal* 28:585, 594 (1961); A. Lee Bradford and Joseph Jennings, "Products Liability Again," *Insurance Counsel Journal* 29: 239, 239 (1962); and S. Weston Burns, "A Defense Lawyer Looks at Products Liability," *Insurance Counsel Journal* 576, 582 (1962).

care expended in its design and manufacture instead of requiring the plaintiff to prove negligence.[98]

Despite the concerns of businesses, their insurers, and their insurers' lawyers, no "product liability crisis" arose until many years after the advent of strict liability in defective product cases. Since businesses passed on the cost of product liability insurance to consumers, insurers profited from these policies, and since the practice of insurance defense was lucrative for insurance lawyers, industry opposition to strict liability for product defects was muted.

While *Greenman* generated little interest outside of legal circles, it provoked much discussion among law professors. Scholarly debate on strict liability gained increasing prominence in law reviews during the sixties. Although very few law reviews mentioned Traynor's *Escola* concurrence before *Greenman,* many law reviews across the country cited and discussed both *Greenman* and *Escola* in the mid-sixties and later. Traynor's strict liability opinions were not so much a conduit for scholarly opinion as G. Edward White has suggested; rather, they preceded most scholarly interest in the subject. Certainly Prosser's Treatise on Torts influenced Traynor's opinion in *Escola,* but even Prosser's most influential articles on strict liability came well after *Escola,* as did most of the scholarly commentary on strict liability. Most of the scholarly commentary on strict liability came after the Restatement (Second) of Torts in 1965. Scholarly opinion was not the impetus for the adoption of strict liability, but a reaction to it.

The 1965 Restatement (Second) of Torts, which influenced so many state courts, closely paralleled Traynor's opinion in *Greenman.* Like other American Law Institute (ALI) restatements of law, it was intended to promote national uniformity in the law, and many judges accepted the Restatement as legal authority, citing it alongside *Greenman* as support for reform. The resemblance of the Restatement to Traynor's thinking on product liability was no surprise since Prosser headed the American Law Institute Committee on tort reform, while Traynor sat as a member of the Committee. In language that would be quoted by numerous other courts, Traynor wrote in *Greenman,* "The purpose of such [strict] liability is to insure that the costs of injuries resulting from defective products are borne by the manufacturers that put such products on the market rather than by the injured persons who are powerless to protect themselves."[99] Section 402A of the Restatement (Second) of Torts followed the same lines of reasoning: "public policy demands the cost of injuries due to defective products be placed on those who market them; and, such injuries are properly treated as a cost of production and insurable risks by those in the best position to seek such

---

[98]Cowie, *"Res Ipsa Loquitur,"* 583, 583–84.
[99]Greenman, 59 Cal.2d at 63.

protection."[100] Traynor influenced judicial thinking on strict liability not only through his opinions in *Greenman* and *Escola,* but also through the ALI's effort to institute strict liability nationally.

Conclusion

According to Melvin Belli, the advent of strict liability was part of a "civil law revolt" in "recognition of man's individual dignity."[101] This "revolt" he wrote, "was court-born, first in jury verdicts, but now . . . maintained by judge trials and sustained by appellate courts."[102] Belli correctly observed that the dynamics of the consumer economy influenced the way juries and judges viewed product liability cases. Juries and judges wished to hold manufacturers accountable for hidden risks to consumers. As a result, they stretched the conventional doctrines that applied to product liability cases. Strict liability broke with legal convention, but it resonated with consumer desires for maximum freedom and minimum responsibility within the marketplace.

The adoption of strict liability in courts across the country signaled a "quiet revolution" in the law.[103] Strict liability initially generated no public controversy and limited scholarly opposition. Despite the significance of *Greenman*'s break with precedent, it was rarely attacked as an activist decision. Judges explicitly adopted the policy justifications enunciated in *Escola* and *Greenman,* and legal scholars explicitly referred to Traynor's "judicial legislation."[104] However, initial criticism of strict liability doctrine dealt more with the intricacies of the doctrine rather than the process by which it became law. The reaction to *Greenman* demonstrated that judicial policymaking consonant with majoritarian values could gain acceptance.

Not until after product liability reform had swept the country did it become controversial. During the 1970s, 1980s, and 1990s, product liability insurance costs for some industries increased so dramatically that many legislatures enacted liability limitations. Fear of rising prices, particularly during times of high

---

[100]Restatement (Second) of Torts, section 402A, 1965.

[101]Melvin Belli, *The Law Revolt: A Summary of Trends in Modern Criminal and Civil Law,* Vol. II (Belleville, Indiana, 1968), 366–67.

[102]*Ibid.* at 367.

[103]Henderson and Eisenberg, "The Quiet Revolution in Products Liability," 479, 483.

[104]See e.g., Thomas Cowan, "Some Policy Basis of Products Liability," *Stanford Law Review* 17:1077, 1081 (1965); Robert Kreminger, "Should Old Judges Reform Society through the Courts?" *Journal of the State Bar* 47:564 (1972); James Henderson, Jr., and Theodore Eisenberg, "The Quiet Revolution in Products Liability: An Empirical Study in Legal Change," *U.C.L.A Law Review* 37:479 (1990).

inflation, fed widespread doubts about the efficacy of product liability litigation. Stories of massive jury verdicts in product liability cases often offended popular notions of individual responsibility. The "product liability crisis" generated a wave of scholarly criticism and legal reform, and it caused consumers to question the costs of the revolution in product liability law.

Traynor recognized that the expansion of product liability could hurt consumers by increasing the cost of consumer goods. For that reason, he advocated "curbs on such potentially inflationary damages as those for pain and suffering."[105] However, the California Court did little during Traynor's tenure to contain the costs associated with product liability litigation. Reform aimed at containing these costs was left to later courts and legislatures. Traynor's successors on the bench had difficulty responding to the consequences of his product liability policies. The "product liability crisis" brought to the surface conflicting notions of consumer responsibility and freedom. While *Greenman* bred little initial opposition, it set the course toward future controversy.

---

[105]Roger Traynor, "The Ways and Means of Defective Products and Strict Liability," *Tennessee Law Review* 32:363, 376 (1965).

CHAPTER SIX

Roger Traynor and His Case for Judicial Activism

Roger Traynor disliked the phrase judicial activism. "As an interpreter, whether of judicial precedent or statutory law, he [the judge] is necessarily an active analyst and not a passive oracle," Traynor wrote. "An actively analytical judge bears no relation to that ill-defined character, the so-called judicial activist."[1] Judicial activism is most easily identified when a judge explicitly departs from legal precedent in favor of his or her sense of justice or social values. Traynor preferred the phrase "judicial creativity" and used that phrase in describing the judges' proper role.[2] Regardless of Traynor's distaste for the vagueness of the phrase judicial activism, he was an activist judge in that he departed from precedent in favor of his conception of the public interest.

Traynor's landmark decisions diverged from legal convention not only in their results, but in their method. Unlike earlier judicial activists who couched their innovations in conventional language, Traynor announced explicitly that he was making public policy. His innovative decisions relied little on precedent. They consisted mainly of policy analysis, and they often drew criticism in the dissents of other Supreme Court justices for that reason. Traynor's innovative opinions often referred to untraditional sources, such as academic writings and policy-oriented studies. He believed that modern times demanded judicial creativity and that modern advances in the social sciences would assist the judge in this task. The judge, he wrote,

[1]Roger Traynor, "The Limits of Judicial Creativity," *Iowa Law Review* 66:1, 2 (1977).
[2]*Ibid.*

must compose his own mind as he leaves antiquated compositions aside to create some fragments of legal order out of disordered masses of new data. There should be modern ways for such a task, in fairness not only to him but to those who must seek out his judgment and abide by his decision.[3]

Like Louis Brandeis, Traynor looked to sources outside the text of the law —and he called on other judges to do the same. In style and content his opinions demonstrated his "modern ways."

Traynor's brand of judicial activism stood out as an extreme in the intellectual history of judging. He was more explicit than Massachusetts Chief Justice Lemuel Shaw, the great nineteenth-century proponent of the "Commonwealth idea," in his advocacy of the "public interest" in judicial innovation.[4] Compared with Justice Benjamin Cardozo, the greatest state court judge of the early twentieth century, Traynor was more willing to abandon legal conventions. Cardozo wrote of judicial innovation:

Obscurity of statute or of precedent or of custom or of morals, or a collision between some or all of them, may leave the law unsettled, and cast a duty upon the courts to declare it retrospectively in the exercise of a power frankly legislative in function.[5]

Although Cardozo's concept of unsettled law bore some resemblance to Traynor's concept of outdated precedent, in practice Traynor was much less tentative than Cardozo in the exercise of his lawmaking duties. Traynor felt great confidence in his ability as a lawmaker, whereas for Cardozo, like most judicial theorists of his era, the role of lawmaker evoked anxiety. "I sought for certainty," Cardozo wrote. "I was oppressed and disheartened when I found that the quest for it was futile."[6] Traynor's remarkable eagerness to formulate policy when he believed that legal precedent no longer adequately served society set him apart from other creative judges.

Criticism of judicial activism has come from various quarters (e.g., Herbert Weschler, the Process School, and Judge Robert Bork), but it can best be understood in terms of three main sets of arguments. First, when judges base their decisions on their personal sense of justice or social values rather than precedent, their decisions become less predictable. Predictability, this argument goes, is essential to a society in which the law is respected. If parties cannot know the rules that govern their conduct because judges constantly change them, they

---

[3]Traynor, "Better Days in Court," 109, 109.
[4]See Leonard W. Levy, *The Law of the Commonwealth and Chief Justice Shaw* (New York, 1957).
[5]Benjamin N. Cardozo, *The Nature of the Judicial Process* (New Haven, 1975), 128.
[6]*Ibid.,* 166.

cannot act according to the rules. By making the law less predictable, judicial activism undermines the law and respect for the law. The second argument is that judicial activism violates democratic principles. When judges go beyond their proper role by making law instead of applying precedent they usurp the policymaking authority of the legislature and politicize the institution of the judiciary. The third argument contends that judges are poorly suited to make policy. They lack the capacity for thorough and consistent policy analysis, assessment, and implementation. Only legislative bodies and executive bureaucracies have the tools to investigate the societal circumstances surrounding a social or economic policy.

Opponents of Traynor's innovative decisions articulated each of the three arguments against judicial activism, and Traynor attempted to answer those arguments. In response to the argument that judicial activism reduced the law's predictability, Traynor contended that inertia was more likely than judicial activism to undermine respect for the law. He was mindful of the need to maintain the stability of the law. "A judge," he wrote,

> coming upon a precedent that he might not himself have established will ordinarily feel impelled to follow it to maintain the stability in the law that has value *per se*. Better the settled precedents that have proved reasonably acceptable and are reasonably in tune with the times than endless re-examinations that create uncertainty without insuring improvement. The serviceable consistency of *stare decisis* rightly discourages the displacement of precedent, absent overwhelming countervailing considerations. It also rightly discourages specious distinctions that confuse more than they clarify.[7]

On the other hand, Traynor wrote, "considerations of the stability of the law alone will lead in the wrong direction," and "overwhelming countervailing considerations" required reconsideration of precedent.[8] In such cases, innovation entailed less risk to the health of the law than did blind adherence to legal convention.

Traynor objected to the continued observance of rules he believed had outlived their original justification. "[W]hen a precedent is outdated," he wrote, "the judge should liquidate it."[9] To overvalue legal certainty by retaining outdated precedents would undermine the law, not shore it up.

The trouble is that the formula (i.e., the law) may encase notions that have never been cleaned and pressed and might disintegrate if they were. We might not accept the formula so readily were we to examine what lies beneath it. We

---

[7] Traynor, "La Rude Vita," 223, 229–30.
[8] *Ibid.*
[9] *Ibid.*

would then learn that its apologists are not defenders of stability as they profess but rationalizers of inertia.[10]

For Traynor the stability of the law depended on its resonance with social conditions. Far from eroding the respect for the law, judicial innovation was essential to the law's health.

Traynor's notion of outdated precedent was central to his justification for judicial activism, but it betrayed the conceptual weakness of his approach. Traynor believed that judges, objectively measuring societal input, would somehow know when a precedent had become outdated. He did not provide guidelines for identifying "outdated" precedent. According to Traynor, the process involved a "value judgment as to what the law ought to be."[11] Paradoxically, this "value judgment" was guided by objective analysis.

Setting aside this conceptual dissonance between judicial "value judgment" and judicial objectivity, Traynor's most innovative decisions succeeded in eliminating precedents that had failed to serve society in some important way. Collusive divorce proceedings, illegal police searches, and unwieldy legal fictions in product liability cases were some of the results of blind adherence to precedent. Traynor's innovative decisions eliminated such practices that circumvented or even violated the law.

Traynor's innovative decisions did cause temporary uncertainty as they became institutionalized. Some of Traynor's policy innovations also helped breed a series of destabilizing legal changes as the doctrinal consequences of his policy rationale unfolded. This was particularly the case with the "divorce revolution" of the early 1970s and the "product liability crisis" of the mid-1970s. Traynor did not intend these developments, and, to a large extent, they were beyond his control. On the other hand, he recognized that judicial innovation could cause legal instability. For him, the benefits of eliminating outdated precedent simply outweighed any risk of legal uncertainty that might result.

Traynor attempted to counteract the destabilizing effect of judicial innovation with legal rules designed to achieve clearly articulated social policy objectives. As Justice Raymond Sullivan, Traynor's colleague on the court, noted, Traynor had a "jurisprudential sense. . . . [H]e looked at the entire scope of the law and saw how it all fitted. He could fit the day to day problems into his broad ideas and concepts."[12] Donald Barrett agreed: "Judge Traynor was particularly concerned with keeping the pattern of the law straight."[13] *Cahan* and the cases

---

[10]Traynor, "Better Days in Court," 109, 161.

[11]Traynor, "La Rude Vita," 223, 234.

[12]Oral History Project: Justice Raymond L. Sullivan, Hastings Sixty Five Club, February 11, 1987, at 21 (Traynor Papers).

[13]Oral History Project: Donald P. Barrett Esq., Senior Attorney, Supreme Court of California 1948–1981, May 28, 1986, July 28, 1986, at 21 (Traynor Papers).

that followed it exemplified his approach; the policy objective of deterring illegal police searches gave coherence to his "workable rules" for police conduct. Traynor attempted to replace the predictability of *stare decisis* with the predictability of coherent social policy.

Traynor believed that the practice of upholding precedents was no more consistent with democratic principles than the practice of occasionally overruling them. Outdated precedent had no greater claim to democratic origins than did the decisions of contemporary judges. "[P]recedents had once to [be] created by an obscure thought process that apparently equates the creativeness of ancient judges with divination," Traynor wrote.[14] Repeated judicial reliance on a precedent did not make it any more democratic. To the contrary, the older the precedent, the greater the risk that it had failed to take into account changing societal conditions. Without judicial innovation, the law might become anachronistic in its treatment of individual freedoms. These anachronisms would threaten democratic values. For Traynor, the threat to democracy came not from judicial decision making, but from judicial passivity.

Traynor believed that judges would not overzealously carry out their duties as lawmakers because most judges were cautious by nature and temperamentally opposed to reform. "[W]e are . . . schooled in the tradition that the law must remain at a respectful distance behind the customs and values of the community," he wrote, "in the main confirming rather than innovating change."[15] Traynor believed that judges were uniquely equipped to institute legal reform precisely because their insulation from political pressure permitted them greater circumspection than legislators. The increasing professionalization of the courts, Traynor further contended, would help ensure that judges had the capacity for thorough, consistent policy analysis, assessment, and implementation. To his credit, Traynor sought to improve the quality of the bench through new selection procedures and continuing professional education. Advocating specialized instruction for judges, he sought to ensure that judges would rise to their responsibilities as lawmakers. He supported the Conference of California Judges seminar program and pushed for the creation of the California College of Trial Judges.[16] He also helped to design a merit plan for the selection of judges.[17] At the 1967 opening session of the College of Trial Judges, he proudly noted that California

---

[14]Traynor, "*Stare Decisis* versus Social Change."

[15]Roger Traynor, "What Doomsday Books for Emerging Law," *Southern California Law Review* 15:1105, 1105 (1968).

[16]Traynor, "Remarks of Chief Justice Roger Traynor," Opening Session, College of Trial Judges.

[17]Roger Traynor, "Good Judges, Good Law," (A dedication of the Earl Warren Legal Center, Boalt Hall, January 2, 1968, Traynor Papers).

had among the most ambitious programs for the education of judges.[18] According to Traynor, the professional ethos of the bench would keep judges from exceeding their authority and violating democratic principles.

Traynor's faith in judicial decision making had a dark side. If judicial detachment and objectivity made judges good lawmakers, then the nature of electoral politics often made legislators bad ones. Traynor believed that the responsibility for legal reform fell too heavily on "the people" and the legislature.[19] He had misgivings about the abilities of legislators.

Too often they legislate madly, confounding the confusions of one paragraph with several more to explain what the first paragraph is deemed to mean if read alone, if read in conjunction with two others, or if read to the famous Welsh treatise on the active and inert elements of a homeless verb.[20]

"What the legislators lacked in skill," Traynor wrote sarcastically, "they made up for in volume."[21] He doubted that legislators were equipped to handle the complexities of reforming the common law. "[A]rriving and departing legislators may have little awareness of the developing problems of the common law," he wrote, "let alone a sense of its continuity."[22] Traynor explicitly disagreed with the "anti-judges" who contended that "the legislators have a unique sensitivity to popular needs or what is sometimes called an ear to the ground."[23] He argued that "we certainly cannot afford now, if we ever could, to play law by ear. . . . [T]here may be little reality to the supposed closeness of a legislator to the needs of all his constituents."[24]

Traynor's strident attack on the legislature in his law review articles contrasted with the cautious approach of his judicial opinions. He had two very different writing styles.[25] His judicial opinions employed the lean, analytical style of policy analysis. His writings off of the bench employed a florid style that highlighted his elitism. In practice, Traynor limited his policymaking to cases of clearly outdated precedent. When he wrote about judicial decision making in law review articles, his justification for judicial activism appeared much more expansive. He sometimes seemed to suggest that the judiciary would be justified in countermanding the legislature whenever it made bad policy. Ironically, his

---

[18]*Ibid.*

[19]Traynor, "Law and Social Change," 230.

[20]Traynor, "The Limits of Judicial Creativity," 1, 24.

[21]*Ibid.*

[22]Traynor, "*Stare Decisis* Versus Social Change."

[23]*Ibid.*

[24]*Ibid.*

[25]The difference between the style of Traynor's opinions and his law review articles is attributable in part to the influence of Madeleine Traynor, who helped write many of his law review articles.

innovative opinions tended not to challenge the wisdom of statutes so much as the wisdom of judicial precedents. Although he did not practice exactly what he preached, his writings reveal the elitism underlying his willingness to make policy. To say the least, Traynor believed that bad public policy—formulated by the legislature, which he distrusted—threatened the public welfare more than the elitism of judicial lawmaking.

According to Traynor, judges were obliged to formulate public policy scientifically, incorporating societal inputs in their decision-making process; they would not undermine democratic principles if they acted in the public interest. Traynor's confidence in the abilities of judges to objectively evaluate societal input went hand in hand with his somewhat naive scientism. He did not appear to see any tension between the scientific process of judicial policy formulation and democratic principles. His belief that objective analysis of "environmental data" enabled judges to determine the public interest made him indifferent to the elitism of his scientific process of policy formation.

A judicial determination of the public interest would not undermine democratic principles if it responded to societal consensus. Traynor believed that societal demands were unified enough to justify his confidence in judicial policymaking. Ironically, Traynor's innovative opinions rarely gained the unanimous support of the other justices, and Traynor himself frequently dissented from the Court's opinions. (He dissented 147 times during his tenure on the bench.) His conception of the public interest often did not generate consensus on the Court because most other justices valued *stare decisis* much more highly than Traynor did. Traynor also overestimated societal consensus in support of his conception of the public interest. Societal attitudes regarding interracial marriage, divorce, criminal justice, and product liability were far more disparate and complex than he recognized. However, Traynor showed extraordinary talent for innovating in those areas without generating controversy. Compared with the public response to the California Supreme Court's decisions to block the death penalty in the 1970s, for example, Traynor's reforms generated relatively little popular reaction. With the exception of his opinion in *Cahan,* even his most innovative opinions did not generate significant public backlash. Traynor and others on the California Supreme Court during Traynor's tenure—particularly Chief Justice Gibson—carefully avoided self-inflicted wounds to the Court. Traynor was aware of the political implications of the Court's actions, and he wrote his opinions with attention to the anticipated response. He eluded controversy by framing his innovative opinions as responses to "weaknesses or disorders" in the law and by carefully avoiding statements of broad principle.[26] However, the muted reaction to Traynor's innovative decisions did not indicate societal consensus so much as societal acquiescence.

---

[26]Traynor, "Better Days in Court," 109, 123.

Although Traynor overestimated societal consensus in support of his conception of the public interest, his innovative decisions did take into account societal input, and they did succeed in addressing some societal demands. They each implicitly or explicitly recognized the societal dynamics revealed in the cases themselves. Traynor acted to reform the law where it preserved power relations that he considered unequal and unfair. He opposed legal rules that perpetuated racial inequality in *Perez* and gender inequality in *DeBurgh*. He acted to protect suspected criminals from excessive police intrusions into their privacy in *Cahan* and its progeny. His product liability opinions attempted to offset the power disparity between producers and consumers. In each of these cases, legal rules had perpetuated the subordination of relatively weak groups of individuals. In Traynor's view, this inequality ran counter to a public interest in individual freedom—be it freedom to marry a spouse of one's choosing, freedom to end an abusive marriage, freedom from illegal police searches, or freedom to exercise consumer choice without assuming unknown risks. While Traynor's confidence in his ability to discern the public interest was fundamentally elitist, egalitarianism was a theme that ran through his innovative opinions.

Opponents of Traynor's activist approach often criticized him for "judicial legislation," not only because they believed he usurped the democratic authority of the legislature, but because they believed judges lacked the tools necessary to formulate social policy. Traynor himself embraced this position when it suited him, notably in cases involving the regulation of labor. "The Legislature is uniquely able to amass economic data and hold hearings where it can give heed to many representatives of the public besides parties to a controversy," he wrote, "It can best determine whether there should be further governmental regulation of peaceful competitive economic activity."[27] Traynor did not feel the same need to "amass economic data" or "hold [public] hearings" in product liability cases, though the economic policy questions raised by product liability cases were no less complex than those involved in labor regulations. Traynor advocated strict liability because, even without amassing the economic data, he believed it to be in the public interest. He simply did not see a public interest in the judicial regulation of union activities, and the essential subjectivity of this choice did not seem to trouble him.

Although they contended that judges lacked the capacity for thorough, consistent policy analysis, critics of Traynor's "judicial legislation" rarely attacked his innovative opinions as bad policy. In *Perez* and *DeBurgh,* the judges who disagreed with Traynor avoided defending the old, outmoded rules, arguing instead that reform was up to the legislature. Initially, *Perez, DeBurgh, Escola,* and *Greenman* generated little substantive criticism. *Cahan* sparked an outcry from law enforcement officers, but the series of cases following it and practical

---

[27]Messner, 53 Cal.2d 873, 890.

experience with the new exclusionary rule tempered substantive criticism of the new policy. Although critics rarely attacked Traynor's innovative opinions as bad policy, the controversy in later years surrounding divorce reform, criminal justice reform, and product liability showed that the value judgments underlying Traynor's policy innovations became hotly contested. The initial lack of controversy surrounding these innovations did not indicate societal consensus that they were good policy. It did demonstrate, however, Traynor's political skill in making reform uncontroversial.

Traynor believed that a new role for judges was gaining acceptance in the post-New Deal Era. "There is now widespread agreement," he wrote, "that a judge can and should participate creatively in the development of the common law."[28] During Traynor's tenure, the California Supreme Court gained a reputation as the most forward-looking and prestigious court in the country, and it became the court most frequently cited by other state Supreme Courts.[29] The adoption of Traynor's policy innovations was not, however, a good measure of the acceptance of Traynor's activist approach. One of the lessons of Legal Realism was that judges necessarily brought their own values to bear on legal questions. According to Traynor and the Realists, a judge's decision not to discard an outdated precedent was simply a value judgment based on a preference for predictability in the law and an aversion to judicial activism. Some of Traynor's policy changes became institutionalized outside of California as judges chose his precedents over older ones. The institutionalization of Traynor's innovations suggested that other judges shared the values expressed in his innovative opinions. It did not indicate a consensus on the bench in favor of an activist approach to judging.

A few courts cited Traynor's innovative opinions in support of their own activist approach.[30] Like the California Supreme Court, courts in a few other states—most notably New Jersey and New York—gained reputations as legal innovators.[31] While Traynor's example certainly provided encouragement to these courts, a new activist role for judges did not gain widespread acceptance. During the Warren era, many state courts resisted the new civil rights jurisprudence imposed on them by the U.S. Supreme Court. At the 1958 meeting of the Conference of Chief Justices, only California's chief justice, Phil Gibson, and

---

[28]Roger Traynor "Comment" on Justice Charles Breitel's "The Courts and Lawmaking" in Monrad G. Paulsen, ed., *Legal Institutions Today and Tomorrow* (New York, 1959), 52.

[29]Friedman, Kagan, Cartwright, and Wheeler, "State Supreme Courts," 773, 805.

[30]See e.g., Baker v. City of Fairbanks 471 P.2d 386 (1970); and Roberts v. State 458 P.2d 340 (1969).

[31]See William Brennan, Jr., "State Constitutions and the Protection of Individual Rights," *Harvard Law Review* 90:489 (1977).

the chief justices of seven other states voted against a resolution calling on the high court to restrain itself from further expanding the application of the Bill of Rights to the states.[32] Even liberals felt apprehensive about judicial lawmaking.[33] The triumph of the New Deal over the conservative Supreme Court and the ascendancy of the Warren Court did not eliminate this apprehension.

On the other hand, the argument that Traynor's innovative decisions usurped legislative prerogative had little if any resonance outside some segments of the legal community. Discourse over judicial activism occurred primarily within the legal community. The public reaction generated by Traynor's innovative opinions had to do more with the substance of his decisions than his activism. *Greenman* and *DeBurgh* changed the legal mechanics of numerous product liability and divorce cases, but these decisions aroused little attention or public debate. *Perez,* on the other hand, affected relatively few people because of the rarity of long-term, open, interracial unions, but it sparked publicity. Unpopular decisions, not judicial activism, stimulated public interest.

The acceptance by other judges of Traynor's innovations corresponded with the strength of societal preferences for and aversions to his policy reforms. *Perez,* a decision that went against strong societal antipathy toward interracial marriage, had little or no impact outside of California. *Cahan,* which generated some public protest, gained a significant following only after the U.S. Supreme Court cited it prominently in support of a federally mandated exclusionary rule. *DeBurgh,* which responded to the persistent demands of spouses in divorce litigation, despite widespread societal aversion to divorce, influenced several state courts outside California, but it played an even more important part in the legislative effort for divorce reform. *Greenman* reflected widespread attitudes toward the risks to consumers of defective products and so gained support in courts across the country. The process of institutionalizing his innovative decisions took different courses, but, with the exception of *Perez,* they gained acceptance, and they did so primarily because societal conditions were amenable to them.

Traynor's innovative opinions often implicated the institutional self-interest of the judiciary by pointing out legal rules that were routinely ignored or circumvented. Until *Greenman,* product liability cases routinely involved the circumvention by courts and juries of the rule of privity of contract. Until the *DeBurgh* decision, judges routinely granted divorces on the basis of the scripted, collusive testimony of spouses. The persistence of illegal police searches despite judicial warnings caused Traynor to feel that a failure to act in *Cahan* would make the judiciary complicitous in police disregard for the Fourth Amendment.

---

[32]"Project Report: Toward an Activist Role for the State Bill of Rights," *Harvard Civil Rights—Civil Liberties Law Review* 8:271, 274 (1973), republished in Paul Murphy, ed., *The Bill of Rights and American Legal History* (New York, 1990).

[33]See Kalman, *The Strange Career of Legal Liberalism.*

Courts outside of California followed these innovative decisions in part because the dysfunction of the old precedents threatened the integrity of the judicial process. *Perez,* by contrast, dealt with a statute that offended the values of many judges on the bench, but which did not embrace a flaw in judicial administration. As a result, *Perez* gained no judicial following outside of California. Along with societal preferences for legal reform, the institutional self-interest of the judiciary weighed in the balance against judges' inclination to adhere to the legal status quo.

Traynor's justification for judicial activism contravened the prevailing legalism of the judges who were his contemporaries, but, at the same time, he provided avenues for other judges to embrace reform. In a stable judicial system not all judges can be innovators. However, to the extent that the stability of the judicial system required responsiveness to societal change, some of Traynor's innovative decisions helped maintain confidence in that system. Their acceptance demonstrated the judicial system's ability to institutionalize judicial innovation.

The "constitutional revolution of 1937," which allowed the expansion of government regulatory power over the economy while creating a new civil liberties jurisprudence, took place in the same ideological environment as Traynor's reform efforts. But although the thrust of Traynor's innovative decisions paralleled this revolution in federal constitutional interpretation, Traynor's efforts at reform generated far less controversy. His brand of activism differed from the activism of the two most prominent activist courts of his era, the conservative U.S. Supreme Court that resisted the New Deal in the early 1930s and the Warren Court or the 1960s; and Traynor's success at gaining institutional acceptance for his judicial innovations depended in part on this difference. Mindful of the lessons of FDR's court packing plan, Traynor tried to avoid political conflict by presenting his legal innovations as corrective and technical. Unlike the conservative Court that resisted the New Deal before 1937 and unlike the Warren Court, Traynor generally did not decide issues of broad constitutional import. Although Traynor and Chief Justice Warren certainly shared a desire to reform the law where it treated certain disadvantaged groups in ways they considered unfair, unlike most of the Warren Court decisions, Traynor's innovative decisions were not enmeshed in the controversy over civil rights.[34] Moreover, even in cases that dealt with the rights of minorities, women, and the criminally ac-

---

[34]When Traynor did take an activist stance in a racially sensitive case, such as *Perez* and *Reitman v. Mulkey,* he did, however, generate controversy. In *Reitman,* when the Court struck down as unconstitutional an initiative (Proposition 14) that prohibited the state from interfering with the right of landlords and home sellers to discriminate on the basis of race, it sparked a movement to oust the justices. Reitman v. Mulkey, 387 U.S 369, 64 Cal.2d 529.

cused, Traynor's opinions focused on the public interest, rather than on group rights. A foundational assumption of his innovative opinions was that Americans were unified enough to share a public interest, and he made the explication of the public interest the centerpiece of his innovative opinions. The activist decisions of the New Deal Court and the Warren Court, on the other hand, tended to focus on the rights of individuals and the powers of government. "Rights talk" was not a significant part of Traynor's rhetoric. To the contrary, his rationalistic style of public policy analysis set apart his brand of judicial activism. It gave his innovative opinions their persuasive force and tempered their potentially controversial implications.

Traynor's career teaches complex lessons. There are valid theoretical objections to his activist approach toward judging, and some of the unintended consequences of his policy innovations raise questions about the wisdom of those innovations. On the other hand, Traynor sought admirably to improve his profession and the health of the law. His innovative opinions committed the law to the equitable treatment of individuals who had relatively little power in society. The egalitarianism of these innovations reflected a vision of social justice that remains attractive today. For Traynor, equality was not only a constitutional principle but also a practical requirement for a harmonious society. He was overly sanguine about the prospects for legal reform and overly optimistic about judicial capacity to accomplish that reform; his legacy has not inspired judicial activism. His enduring achievement has been the widespread influence of his articulation of the public interest.